First edition published September 2020

Interior: Jill Kanter

Cover: Theresa Barzyk

With gratitude to my friend who prodded me into presenting my experiences as the wellspring of my ideas.

A Hacker's Teleology: Sharing the Wealth of Our Shrinking Planet

Charles Hugh Smith

TABLE OF CONTENTS

Introduction

While it's natural to mourn the end of an era, no matter how unsustainable it might have been, it's energizing to enter a new era.

While we don't know the future, we do know that the previous arrangement was failing even before the global upheavals. The unearned privileges of wealthy insiders had pushed unfairness and inequality to precarious extremes, and perverse incentives pushed over-consumption and debt to equally unstable extremes. We now have an once-in-a-lifetime opportunity to launch a new arrangement that works for everyone, not just the few insiders at the top of a corrupt heap.

The previous arrangement--our *socio-economic system* for lack of a better phrase--was not sustainable, and so its demise was inevitable. To organize all of human life around the conviction that infinite growth was possible on a planet figuratively shrinking in resources was never anything but a vain fantasy. To organize the destruction of the planet in the pursuit of infinite growth so insiders could make even more money—that scheme was disconnected from reality.

The solution will not be a grand "ism" that promises a utopian perfection that ends up enslaving us all. Nor will the solution be some version of Central Planning—by its very nature, an arrangement that favors the few at the expense of the many—under some noble-sounding slogan.

The solution will be a human-scale, messy infinity of opportunity to make incremental advances, one person and one step at a time. Not every step will be a success; many will be experiments that fail, but since we learn far more from failure than success, this pursuit of small improvements in well-being and sustainability will be a form of progress that's open to everyone.

This will require more than a new arrangement of people, capital and governance; it will require a new set of shared values and a new definition of progress.

Stripped of niceties, the old definition of success was: we must consume more, regardless of the destructive consequences, and borrow more money to pay for consuming more, because infinite growth makes everyone happy and somebody somewhere—usually someone far away—will make fantastic amounts of money.

Infinitely increasing consumption and debt was never sustainable, and consuming more didn't deliver the promised universal happiness. The corrupt values buried in this arrangement—which we can summarize as *anything goes for the rich and powerful and winner takes all*—were equally unsustainable.

These values were artfully hidden by a vision of a utopian technological wonderland where machines and computers did all the work and we luxuriated in their embrace while the few who owned the wonderland became immensely rich. This too was doomed, for it was never anything but a shinier version of *winner takes all*.

A more sustainable and humane definition of progress is: advancing well-being and sustainability in small, incremental steps with fewer resources, not more; relying not on ever-increasing debt but on increasing productive opportunities for the many rather than just for the few.

Everyone who benefited from the old broken arrangements will naturally try to restore the good old days of more consumption making a few insiders even more gloriously rich, even as the tide has turned irrevocably against them. As a result, attempts to reform the system from within will be watered down by the entrenched interests trying to reverse the tides of time. They will fail to reverse these tides, but they will easily crush any reforms that threaten their feeding trough.

To share the wealth of our shrinking planet, we need a *Hacker's Teleology*—a set of goals, tools and values that work around all the Old Guard's broken systems to reach new solutions quickly and effectively. That's the goal of this book: to propose a new arrangement that provides a sustainable wealth of opportunities for all.

The road doesn't always go where we think it will, but fortunately the lives we've led give us sufficient tools to deal with change, both in our own lives and in our global civilization. The option to *not* change no longer exists; the unsustainable era has reached its inevitable end. A new era beckons, and with what we already have in hand we can forge a more sustainable, healthier, fairer and more productive alternative.

Section One:
Connecting the Dots

The blueprint for a more sustainable, productive arrangement seems obvious to me, but since many of its features are unique to my work, it's clear that this blueprint may not be as obvious to everyone else.

Each of us has a wealth of experiences that are as unique as our fingerprints. These experiences are the seeds of our understanding and insight. Though life experiences are unique to each individual, the drives and desires that generate experiences are universal to all humans: we all want to belong to something larger than ourselves, to be valued, to contribute, and to fulfill our ambitions.

Okay, Mr. Author, you ask, just how did your experiences lead to a blueprint for *sharing the wealth of a shrinking planet*? The answer comes from Steve Jobs' timeless 2005 commencement speech at Stanford University, in which he described how seemingly unrelated experiences gave him the tools needed to launch Apple with his friend Steve Wozniak.

Jobs' point was that *each of us shares this story:* experiences that don't seem connected—successes, major flops, dead-ends, and everything in between—actually do connect up when we've assembled the experiences needed to advance. How our successes, flops and dead-ends all tie together is only visible after they connect. In Job's words, *"You can't connect the dots looking forward; you can only connect them looking backward."*
One way to understand Jobs' point is to ask: what experiences were absolutely necessary for me to advance from A to B to C? What advances *would have been impossible if I hadn't had these specific experiences*? For Jobs, one such experience was a calligraphy / typography class at Reed College, a course that appeared utterly impractical at the time but which led a decade later to the Macintosh computer's revolutionary menu of fonts.

One of the unspoken lessons of Jobs' speech is that *unconventional experiences lend themselves to unconventional solutions*. Before Jobs co-founded Apple, no one could have predicted his astounding success based on his jumble of experiences (college dropout, working in an apple orchard, etc.). Yet that jumble was, by his own account, key to his success in impossible-to-predict ways.

This runs counter to the conventional track: earn a college diploma, add an advanced professional degree, and build a career in a specialized field. Any counselor who recommended dropping out of college to assemble a jumble of unconventional experiences would be run out of town as a corruptor of youth.

There is a thread connecting all of Jobs' experiences that he didn't mention: *authenticity*. In pursuing each experience, he was being true to himself and his enthusiasms. It wasn't a random jumble, it was guided by his inner compass of what inspired him. By his own account, he wasn't tending apple trees because he had to—he loved the work and returned to the orchard when the opportunity arose.

All of us have experienced the *rightness of being true to ourselves*. Once again, Jobs' story is *our story*: none of our successes come from living someone else's life, and few advances of human endeavor come from dogmatically following conventions. Rather, advances come from people who have *no choice but to pursue their enthusiasms with unrelenting intensity*. They do this not because somebody told them to; they literally have no other choice.

Which brings us to Jobs' final point: life is short, so do you want to spend your life doing work you don't care about? In his words, *"The only way to do great work is to love what you do. Your time is limited, so don't waste it living someone else's life. Don't be trapped by dogma — which is living with the results of other people's thinking."*

Conventions and dogma don't just distract us from our true selves; they also lead to getting things completely wrong when events don't follow the conventional script.

The Global Financial Crisis of 2008-09 is a recent example of conventional dogma being a catastrophically poor guide. Virtually all the highly credentialed economic experts got it completely wrong: their models didn't reflect the financial system as it actually functioned and so they underestimated the risks of contagion. As the wildfire spread to the entire global financial system, they continued to assure the public that the fire was contained and all was well.

The conventional dogma failed, and by at least some measures, continues to fail, as the policies of the past decade haven't fixed what's broken.

Many of us outside the mainstream recognized the risks of a crash were rising. It didn't require any special expertise to reach this conclusion; those of us with real-world experience could see the system was broken, and *doing more of the same* was only increasing the risk of a breakdown.

The current arrangement—*our socio-economic-political system*—no longer works for the many; it only works for the few. It's broken, and while the mainstream holds that it can be fixed by replacing a few bits here and there and borrowing a few more trillion dollars, it's not just the rusty bits that are broken: the entire foundation is cracking apart. Even those who aren't versed in economics feel this in their bones.

Those who are doing well don't see what's broken; from their perch, *the system works for me so it must work for everyone else*. But when the foundations crack, even the wealthy and powerful will lose. The story of the foundations cracking isn't just *my story; it's our story*, for we all live in the same system.

You've probably guessed that my experiences haven't followed a conventional line. Most of my life can be summarized as *fools rush in*: short of training, money and mentors, I've taken longshots, pursued impractical studies, and predictably made very little money. At nineteen I received a couple hundred dollars and a rusty Volkswagen Beetle in need of an engine rebuild, and that was my total starting capital.

Here's my dot-connecting: my experiences led me to ask big questions about how we can *share the wealth of a shrinking planet* and seek big, comprehensive answers.

There's a word for the dot-connecting Steve Jobs described: *teleology*. It's a fancy word that means *where it all leads to*. It's not just a goal, it's *the destination we end up reaching because that's where the connected dots lead*.

My teleology led me to ask: is there a better way to live, one that uses Earth's resources more wisely? What about *our system* locks us into such a wasteful, precarious, perverse, unsustainable way of life? Is there an alternative arrangement that would create a more sustainable, better way of life for everyone, and if so, what would it look like?

In the context of computers, *hacker* refers to someone who breaks into a system with malicious intent. But the original meaning of a *hack* is a work-around in a kludgy system that we don't have the time or money to rebuild from scratch; hence the term *life-hack* for a handy shortcut or work-around.

So when I refer to a *hacker's teleology*, I mean a *teleology of workarounds* in a kludgy system that can't be reformed because insiders have locked it so it can't be changed. This makes perfect sense: why would those in charge risk modifying a system that's rewarded them so well?

While the experiences recounted here are part of *my story*, this book is actually about *our story*, too, for we all inhabit the same planet, and all our experiences ultimately connect to the broken system we share.

Just as there are dots connecting our life experiences, there are dots connecting the system's broken *that-grinding-doesn't-sound-good* parts, and dots connecting my experiences to my vision of an alternative way to share a shrinking planet. And just as there is a dot-connecting teleology in our own lives, the *hacker's teleology* connects the dots of *values, processes and systems*. Let's get started!

Section Two:
Belonging

The old wooden gym echoed with the sound of bouncing basketballs and I glanced up at the afternoon sun filtering through the half-open windows high above the stands. Lanai's gym was 2,500 miles and a world away from the California mountain town I'd left a few weeks before, but the initial disorientation was slowly fading, thanks to being on the varsity basketball squad.

It seemed like just another practice until one of my teammates paused the drill and shouted at me in a voice that stopped me cold.

"You think you're better than us?"

My teammate's accusation caught me off-guard, and as he continued in the same charged tone, I flushed under the uneasy gaze of the rest of the team. I wasn't just the only 15-year old new kid in town; I was the only rail-thin, pale, red-haired boy on the team and in the entire high school.

Desperation is not too strong a word for what I felt. Sure, the accusation was unfair, but that didn't matter. What mattered was that I didn't lose the good-will of my teammates. With no friends and no other way to connect with classmates, a place on the team was the one positive in my life. Perhaps only those who have been friendless and alone can understand this desperation and the great human misery of not belonging.

The practice drifted to a stop and I knew my response could save my slot on the team or end it. My teammate had never expressed any ill-will toward me before, and I was mystified what had caused him to take my shy reserve for aloof superiority. It certainly wasn't anything I'd said, because I'd said nothing.

Though I didn't understand what triggered his outburst, it was self-evidently related to my pale skin. As an FOB (fresh-off-the-boat) Mainland *haole*, I knew very little of Hawaii's history, but I'd already gathered that *haoles* (*foreigner* in Hawaiian, but now the local pidgin word for Caucasians) were privileged, a legacy of Hawaii's colonial history, a past reflected in the town's *Haole Hill* where the plantation managers lived.

But I didn't live on *Haole Hill*; we lived in decrepit State teacher housing, which had enough cracks around the windows to welcome every insect from fist-sized field spiders to hundreds of the little fruit beetles that fed on the plantation's decaying pineapples.

Looking back, my teammate's charge was more than a little ironic: here I was, the new kid in town, hyper-conscious of standing apart from my Asian-American and native-Hawaiian classmates, with no friends, struggling to comprehend the island's pidgin English, feeling alone and lost, and I'm accused of feeling superior? And why? For being quiet because I didn't know any other way to be? But how could my teammates know that? Maybe *haole silence = arrogance* was a reasonable assumption.

To defuse the accusation, I stammered the only defense I could think of, saying, no, I don't think I'm superior, I'm the worst player on the team, which was stating the obvious. Though I was a few inches taller than my classmates, compared to them I was a midget in athleticism, skills and experience. I did my best to practice hard, but I had none of my teammates' athletic abilities.

To my relief, this cooled my teammate's ire, and the topic never came up again; eventually my teammates began joking about their *Hawaiian haole*. But the incident stayed with me because of the irony: all I wanted was to belong, while my teammates had the *privilege of belonging* without even being aware of its value. No matter how welcoming my classmates were, a new-kid-in-town *haole* would never really belong in the same way. So who was privileged? The only privilege I wanted was being accepted by my teammates.

Eight months later the school year ended and I was the only *haole* on another team, a crew of 16-year olds picking pineapples in the sweltering summer. There's no shade in a field of pineapples, and the tropic heat blasted us until the sun mercifully set. As a swing-shift crew, we ended our shift at night, working under eerie spot lights strung on the lumbering harvesting boom and truck.

The other boys were from the class one year behind me, and once again I was uncertain of my standing. On the first day, bouncing over the dirt roads in the back of a truck, the wood bin smelling of sickly-sweet pineapple juice, I hoped to earn a place on the crew.

The thorny pineapple plant is hazardous to the eyes and skin, so we all wore goggles, gloves and heavy denim clothing which increased our sweat-soaked discomfort and the risk of heat stroke. Being fair-skinned, all the protective gear kept me from being sunburned, a necessary tradeoff if I was going to work in the sun every day.

I took my place behind the long boom and the conveyor belt started moving with a deafening clatter. The truck carrying the boom assembly lurched forward and we started our eight-hour walk down the endless rows, removing the thorny crown by either twisting it off or slamming the crown against the boom so the fruit tumbled onto the conveyor. Sloppy work that damaged the fruit brought quick reprimands from our middle-aged crew boss (*Luna*).

The management had devised an incentive system based on the expected yield of each field: if a crew was expected to harvest 10 bins and they managed to fill 12, the crew earned a bonus for the extra bins. On a good week, our minimum-wage paychecks could swell by a third if we consistently earned a daily bonus. Any slacker would hurt the entire crew's chances for a bonus, and so I had a double-incentive to keep up.

Even with the advantages of youth, our forearms and wrists ached and we hoped for a brief respite between trucks or an older field with fewer, smaller fruits. (The smaller the fruit, the more difficult the crown was to remove, so it was a mixed blessing.)

Decades later, a classmate told me a story about a fast-food restaurant job he held while attending college in Honolulu. One of his fellow employees was nearly weeping at the difficulty of mopping the tiled floor, and my friend had to restrain a laugh at the relative ease of mopping a floor in an air-conditioned fast-food outlet compared to walking for miles in the blazing heat picking heavy pineapples.

Amidst the usual chatter of 16-year old males during breaks—crude jokes and playful insults—some private jibe must have gone too far, because one of the crew pulled a hunting knife on a fellow crewmember. Sensing the potential for a testosterone-fueled over-reaction, the rest of the crew fell silent.

From my perspective, what was noteworthy about the flare-up—soon calmed by our Filipino *Luna*—was that the knife wasn't pulled on *me*. I no longer stood out; I was part of the background, just another local student on the crew. Even though I would never really belong, *equal effort brought equal respect*. Everyone knew the work was hard, and everyone knew who was doing their best. I'd earned a place on the crew, and a source of pride.

But then all of the connections I'd made on Lanai were lost a few weeks later when I was once again the new kid in town, this time as an incoming senior at Punahou School in Honolulu, the most prestigious of Hawaii's numerous private schools. If working-class plantation Lanai occupied one end of the socio-economic spectrum, Punahou took pride of place at the other end: founded by missionaries in 1841, the oldest school west of the Rockies, Punahou was a bastion of privilege and academic rigor. In a word, *daunting*, especially to an incoming senior without a single social contact and no special scholastic abilities.

I remember sitting on a stone bench on my first day on campus, awaiting my first class with dread, feeling completely out of my depth: the manicured campus, more like a college than a high school, covered an expanse of prime Manoa Valley real estate with athletic fields, teacher housing on Rocky Hill, a classic President's Home and an architectural gem of a chapel fronting a spring.

It also seemed that every one of my 400 classmates was good-looking, confident, gifted, socially adept and rich—and a terrific athlete, artist and musician to boot. Whatever I'd mustered to navigate my year on Lanai didn't apply here, and not only was I literally lost on campus, I was keenly aware that I didn't fit in.

It would have been a lot easier if there had been a *Misfits Club* among the dozens of campus clubs, but alas, no; those of us who didn't fit in had no way to find each other. High school being a cauldron of insecurities, a great many of my classmates might have felt qualified to join a Misfits Club at one time or another; but the real misfits like me would have been wary of joining for fear they wouldn't measure up even as a misfit.

The path to Punahou for the majority of my classmates and their families was arduous; heavy sacrifices were required to save up the tuition (equal to private college tuition) and prospective students had to study hard to gain admittance. Merely being a good student wasn't always enough; excellence in athletics, music or the arts was expected, along with some form of community service. I'd been admitted since my stepfather had joined the faculty and my public-school grades were good, but it was an open question if I could cut it academically.

Given that Punahou was an athletic powerhouse in virtually all competitive sports, making the basketball team was a challenge. I didn't make it on the top AA varsity squad, but managed to just make the cut for the A-level squad. The program was tough—two daily practices instead of the usual one—but I managed, riding my old 3-speed bicycle down Manoa Valley in the dawn rain to the morning practice.

Despite giving it my all, I never connected with any of my teammates. It certainly wasn't the fault of my fellow athletes. Was I just not in the same social league as my classmates? Or was it simply that everyone else already had a circle of friends? For whatever reason, I never really belonged; decades later, while I can remember the names and faces of every one of my Lanai

High teammates, I can't recall a single name of my Punahou classmates, and I doubt any of them remember me, either: I was a non-entity.

Though I never belonged to any formal campus club, belonging to Punahou, even as a misfit, taught me something extremely valuable: *expectations of excellence and open competition bring out the best in us.* When the *less than gifted* manage through discipline to work up to average, we achieve far more than the gifted student who succeeds all too easily. An honest, hard-earned C grade is a much greater accomplishment than an easy A, and there's no substitute for the confidence gained by overcoming obstacles with diligent effort. Knowing our limits helps us to channel our efforts into what we're enthusiastic about—a process that benefits us and whatever project we're pursuing.

In other words, we want to belong not just for the sake of belonging, but to find our best selves and our place in the sun, where we can fulfill our talents and enthusiasms—what we call *getting ahead.*

Belonging Is an Unappreciated Form of Wealth

If we ask, "why do we want to belong?," the short answer is "humans are social animals." But this doesn't really explain our need to belong or the complicated nature of belonging, so let's look at the forms of belonging that don't even occur to us because we take them for granted.

Following Steve Jobs' dictum that we can only connect the dots looking back, the best way to understand belonging is to look back at times when we didn't belong, and what became possible when we did find some way to belong.

The first thing we should note is that *belonging is a privilege, not a right.* Rights are granted to everyone, but privileges are only granted to members in good standing. Rights cannot be wiped out except by legal action, but membership is a choice both for the individual and the group the individual wants to join.

The second thing is that belonging *gives us an identity* beyond what we have an individual. We always retain our own identity, but we gain something by belonging to a team or organization that *reflects our authentic self*: our world expands, and so does our role in that world.

The third thing is that we want to belong to *something larger than ourselves,* something with a meaningful purpose, something that *we actively contribute to* so that *our contribution is valued.* To understand this, let's go back to my intense desire to be part of the Lanai High basketball squad.

Let's imagine that I was offered an alternative to joining the basketball team: if I shot baskets alone at home, I'd be paid $60 a week, the same amount I earned picking pineapple on my summer job (that's about $450 today.)

Obviously the money would be attractive, as it could be used to buy all sorts of stuff I might want. But consider *what the money couldn't buy*: it couldn't buy me what I really wanted, which was a treasured spot on the basketball team, nor could it buy me a way to advance—a process we call *getting ahead*.

So I could remain lonely, disconnected, miserable, with no way to expand my world or contribute—in other words, no way to *get ahead*—and get money that could buy stuff that couldn't possibly substitute for what I lacked: an opportunity to become a better player and be valued as a contributor to the team.

Yes, I might get better at free throws if I took the money and shot baskets alone. But this advance would have been illusory, because we only become a better player by actually playing on a team. As the Taoist philosopher Zhuangzi (also known as Chuang Tzu) noted 2,500 years ago, shooting arrows at a target in calm conditions with nothing on the line is one thing, but shooting arrows when the stakes are high and the pressure is on is another.

Not only that, but being on the team is so much more than an occasional chance to shoot a basket. Being on a team is all about discipline, hard work, sportsmanship, sacrifice and selflessness, and learning from your coach and peers. Some poor kid shooting baskets alone gets none of this. He is impoverished, no matter how much money he gets.

Although it's not recognized as such, belonging is a form of wealth that can't be bought with mere money. Yes, we all need money to live, but we need more than money to live, too. We need opportunities to express our authentic selves in a group where our efforts have value and our sacrifices are respected, where we can earn dignity--something that money can't buy. As noted above, we want an opportunity to develop our best selves and find our place in the sun, where we can fulfill our talents and interests.

Looking back at my experience in Punahou, there's a fourth thing we should note: the kid shooting baskets alone doesn't have any competition. There's nobody guarding him, and nobody to notice or care whether he gets better or not. As I said earlier: *expectations of excellence and open competition bring out the best in us.* Getting "free money" as an isolated individual doesn't give us those opportunities to excel; only belonging gives us those opportunities.

Yet opportunities to belong to something meaningful that give us ways to get ahead are not guaranteed in our economic system. At best it's hit or miss; misfits like myself may never find anything to belong to that offers *gainful employment* (defined as paid work that benefits both the individual and the community) and when the economy slows, opportunities vanish like mist in Death Valley. At worst, the system squanders human talent and resources that could have been put to better use, and leaves millions miserable in dead-end jobs with no way to get ahead. Why do we tolerate such a wasteful, ineffective system?

This raises a question few ask: what if we designed a workaround (i.e. a *hacker's teleology)* that guaranteed everyone opportunities to belong to something purposeful as well as *gainful employment*—i.e. a pathway to *get ahead*?

One final thing that's so obvious we don't really notice its importance is that *some forms of belonging have purposes with an economic value and some don't.*

The basketball team has many purposes—representing the school, entering athletic competitions, fostering teamwork, an opportunity for students to advance their skills, to name a few—but the *primary organizing purpose* isn't making a financial profit. The purposes are social and educational, not financial.

In the current system, work devoted to making someone a profit is paid, and most work with a social gain isn't paid. Depending on the *primary organizing purpose*, even work that produces economic value isn't necessarily paid.

This raises another question few ask: what if all work that *created value* was paid, rather than just the work that made someone a profit or what the government saw fit to pay for? In other words, what if we had a system that guaranteed everyone opportunities to belong to something purposeful that offered every participant gainful employment?

What would that system look like if it was a *workaround* to the wasteful hit-or-miss system we have now?

Belonging, Being Rooted, Being Yourself

There's one more important point about the value of belonging that few (if any) seem to understand. When you feel that you belong, I mean really belong in the sense that it feels right, you feel *rooted* in the place and the organization: it all feels right because you're being valued for *who you really are*, rather than being little more than an interchangeable human robot.

Psychologist Eric Fromm concluded that feeling rooted was essential to human happiness and fulfillment. We tend to associate this sense of being rooted with having deep ties to a place where your family has lived for generations. This is certainly one important kind of rootedness, but the kind I'm describing here isn't dependent on a long history in one place; it's feeling rooted in a group because you're contributing something of your real self which is valued by other members.

In other words, we feel rooted when we belong to something creating real value in the real world—a measurable kind of value—and when we're expressing something of our best self that *advances* the group's work and our own development—what I'm calling *getting ahead*.

What's important is that the positive feelings of belonging, being rooted and being yourself benefit both the individual, who feels happy being valued while making progress in their own lives, and the group, which is far more productive than organizations filled with interchangeable human robots who feel miserable because they're not valued and they're not getting ahead.

A team in which every player feels enthused is much more likely to accomplish great things than a team of dispirited players are just going through the motions.

Similarly, workers who feel valued are much more likely to accomplish great things than workers who know they're interchangeable cogs in an uncaring machine.

When we find something to belong to, we experience a feeling of fulfillment which isn't created by "free money" (the kid paid to shoot baskets alone) or a dead-end job. Contributing to something good (and maybe even something great) creates so much more value than being little more than interchangeable human robots doing dead-end work.

There's one final point to emphasize: *money is not a substitute for belonging and rootedness*. We tell ourselves the money is what matters because the emptiness of our work is too painful to dwell on. But just as the money paid to the kid shooting baskets alone is no substitute for belonging to a team, just making money—even lots of money—cannot create the happiness and fulfillment of being valued for what we contribute.

Why should we settle for a system with so few opportunities to belong, when belonging and being rooted generate much greater human happiness and more productive organizations?

As we set out to design a system that's sole purpose is to create these opportunities for everyone, let's first envision what it would look like.

Section Three:
Getting Ahead

Mentors and Mastery

While belonging gives us a chance to bond with peers (teammates, etc.), it also gives us access to leaders—teachers, bosses, coaches—who can mentor us in ways that our peers cannot. Strong mentors are an important key to getting ahead, which requires *gaining mastery of a productive skill* and an *economic ecosystem*—the tools, allies and networks—needed to put those skills to good use in *gainful employment*.

For many of us, mentors have been scarce. I'll mention three I lucked into: a public school teacher (Burk Bagley); a boss (Dennis Vennen); and a community organization leader (Colin Bell).

That our English teacher Burk Bagley had a prosthetic lower leg was an open secret among the students on Lanai. Like everyone else, I was curious about Mr. Bagley's partially missing limb (lost in a motorcycle accident I learned later), which had no visible effect other than a slight lag in his gait due to the prosthetic's fixed ankle. Even without the mysterious prosthesis, he cut an unusual figure on the plantation town's elementary and high school campus: towering over everyone else at 6 foot 4 inches in height and built like a linebacker, he wore tweed jackets despite the tropic climate.

Though Burk was only 29, about the age of our counterculture heroes John Lennon and Bob Dylan (whose first album Burk lent my brother and I), he seemed two generations older and wiser than us. Despite the age gap, we shared a number of interests other than popular music: Burk rode a big Honda motorcycle to work, and I rode my stepfather's vintage 500 cc Matchless motorcycle when given the chance; Burk was unconventional (he and his wife Martha drove an Austin-Healey sports car and lived in the island's tiny harbor community rather than in town) and he was enthusiastic about teaching and literature. For all these reasons, he was an inspiration not just to me but to other classmates like my friend Colbert Matsumoto.

It was natural for Burk and I to become friends outside the classroom, and he invited my brother and me to visit his tidy rented cottage that overlooked the island's small harbor. We were suitably impressed with his expansive record and book collections, and with a glimpse of his artificial foot when he removed his wingtip shoes.

It was also natural for Colbert and me to ask Burk to be our advisor when we launched our unauthorized (i.e. *underground*) school newspaper, *The Cop-Out*.

Though I couldn't bring myself to share my secret ambition directly—to be a writer like my Existentialist heroes and heroines Simone De Beauvoir, Jean-Paul Sartre and Albert Camus—I hesitantly handed Burk several hand-written stories I'd composed, and his positive response was the first encouragement I ever received to pursue the fantasy of becoming a writer. The chances of success were so remote and the odds of being ridiculed so high that this ambition remained a tightly held secret.

But this encouragement was enough for Colbert and me to launch *The Cop-Out*, which was the start of my writing career. Although I didn't understand it at the time, this single-sheet, two-page, underground school newspaper crammed with articles, student-written poems, and letters to the editor created forms of belonging that are universal to every media outlet.

The Cop-Out belonged to us, but perhaps more importantly, we belonged to *The Cop-Out*, and so did every student whose work we published and every student who read it, in some small but meaningful way. Identifying with a media outlet is a form of belonging: what we contribute to and read expresses who we are and bonds us to other contributors and readers. This is the exact same model of my blog *Of Two Minds*, except the scale has been magnified from a few dozen readers in one school to thousands of readers and millions of page views.

Though it was crudely produced mimeographed pages, *The Cop-Out* had all the processes and tasks of larger media operations. Colbert and I had deadlines for writing, editing, production, distribution and the collection of letters and poems submitted by students. Though no money changed hands, it was just as much an enterprise as any for-profit venture.

Colbert and I didn't join something that already existed--we created it. I didn't grasp the importance of this at the time: if there is no opportunity for belonging to something that expands our interests and abilities—i.e. *getting ahead*—then we can create it ourselves, if the *economic ecosystem*—tools, connections and mentors--are at hand. (I discuss *economic ecosystems* in the next section.)

I didn't appreciate it as an inexperienced 16-year old, but there really wasn't much difference between the unpaid jobs we did on *The Cop-Out*—a complex enterprise in all but name—and getting paid for doing similar kinds of work in a government agency or for-profit company. Eventually it struck me that work and belonging are very much the same whether we're paid or not.

My first formal jobs at Dole Pineapple on Lanai and at the touristy Paradise Park in Honolulu's Manoa Valley, affectionately known as *Parasite Park* by us low-level employees, did not yield any mentors.

Seeking higher pay, I quit Paradise Park and was hired by a new contracting partnership. Dennis Vennen and his then-partner Bill Dixon were my first small-business bosses, and after they went their separate ways, I stayed on with Denny and his new partner Dan Moore while I worked my way through my last two years at the University of Hawaii-Manoa.

Since I was on my own at 19, I was always scrounging for work on the weekends to earn a few more dollars. Denny and his wife owned a 1950s-era fixer-upper ranch house in Kailua with a patio and swimming pool, and Denny asked if I'd be willing to take on an arduous task one weekend: sanding and filling the numerous cracks in the badly leaking pool. He'd drained the pool, and the cracks had to be sanded smooth with a power grinding wheel which spun off clouds of dust and ear-shattering noise that reverberated inside the kidney-shaped pool. With no breeze to dissipate the dust or the mid-day heat, it was hot, uncomfortable work, as I had to wear a heavy dust mask, goggles and a hat.

Denny had been a Navy diver in the Vietnam War, and was now pursuing his entrepreneurial ambitions, backed by an MBA earned after his Navy service. Medium height, always neatly groomed, fit and brimming with energy, Denny had a ready smile and a relaxed sense of humor. He was a good mentor not so much with advice but by his own example: a devoted family man, a hard worker, fair and honest, and able to see past my long unkempt mane of red hair and counterculture views to value what actually mattered: my work ethic and bottomless appetite for learning the building trades and the contracting business.

By the end of the day, I'd finished grinding down all the pool cracks, and favorably impressed Denny with my perseverance at a miserable task.

I doubt many other contractors would have allowed me to change my work schedule every semester so I could maintain a full schedule of five classes, but Denny supported my university education, though he would kid me good-naturedly about majoring in philosophy.

Belonging to Denny and Dan's company, Island Trends, was a four-year master class in building and contracting due to their mentoring. By the time I started my own general contracting company a few years later at age 27, I'd accumulated an irreplaceable trove of experiences to help me navigate the challenges of running a fast-growing contracting business with my partner, Mike Tanner.

Though Island Trends was ultimately unsuccessful financially, and Denny and Dan went their separate ways, their partnership was successful in many other ways, including mentoring me, for I now had the necessary building blocks to *get ahead*.

At 70 years of age, Colin Bell was a very old man to a 20-year old like me. Short, stocky, balding and sporting a gray goatee, Colin looked distinguished, an impression strengthened once he spoke, for his clipped English accent remained despite living in the U.S. since the end of World War II, and his voice expressed his warmth and infectious enthusiasm for life. Measured in liveliness, Colin was still young. As an English Quaker and active member of the faith's "action organization," The Friends Service Committee, Colin had volunteered to be an ambulance driver in World War II and in 1943 had made his way to war-torn China to head up a surgical team in an ambulance unit.

The Friends did not differentiate between combatants; they pursued the Christian ideal of alleviating the suffering of civilians and combatants alike. In the course of his service in China, Colin had met Chou En-Lai and other future leaders of the People's Republic of China when they were a ragged band of Communist insurgents. But more remarkable than his brushes with the future leaders of China was his survival in extremely dangerous conditions: disease took as heavy a toll as bullets.

Given his adventurous life and valorous service to Christian ideals, it was a given that I was in awe of Colin. While many of us professed these ideals, he'd actually lived them, willingly accepting danger and hardship. This was my own ideal: not to just study the world in a classroom or watch from the sidelines, but to take action.

As a newly minted subcommittee chair in the Honolulu branch of the American Friends Service Committee (AFSC), I was supposed to be early for the meeting, which was held in the old open-air carport of the Friends' meeting house in Manoa valley. A cramped white-painted room at the back of the carport served as the AFSC office, with just enough space for the director's desk (big title, poverty-level pay) and a few filing cabinets. Everyone else was a volunteer like me.

But I wasn't early, or even on time. I was late, and not by just a few minutes. The annoyed expressions of the other committee members telegraphed their displeasure with my irresponsibility, and I tried to dissipate the dour mood with a half-hearted joke about it being OK to be late sometimes.

To my mortified surprise, Colin ripped me up one side and down the other. No, it was not OK to be late, it was never OK to keep other members waiting. I'd never seen him angry, for it took a lot to burn through his amiable persona, and I reddened with shame under his dressing down. My cavalier attitude incensed Colin because I wasn't taking my work at AFSC seriously, and the work was worthy of the utmost seriousness and dedication. It wasn't acceptable to waste the precious time of other volunteers, and there was no excuse for my tardiness.

Thoroughly chastened, I mumbled an apology and started the meeting. Without even being aware of it, I'd set my work at AFSC—and yes, it was work, in every sense of the word—in a different category than my construction job because one was paid and the other was not. Since I wasn't being paid, I was cavalier about my responsibilities at AFSC.

Colin did me a great favor by breaking down that assumption. Unpaid work is just as important as paid work, even though we don't measure it in dollars. Purposeful work is valuable, whether it's paid or not. There is no difference in the positive results of good work, paid or unpaid.

Looking back, I realize that Colin's mentoring was not just in the practicalities of running meetings and organizing projects, but in *the moral foundations of belonging and work*: there is a moral obligation to treat all purposeful work seriously, with the utmost dedication, whether you are paid or not. If your commitment to the team or group is half-hearted, you've let everyone down—including yourself.

Economic Ecosystems

Children are constantly told "you can be anything you want to be" as a form of encouragement, but the reality is that starting something new requires more than stardust ambitions. It requires a network of contacts and mentors (what we call *social capital*), a pathway to the experience needed to gain skills (*human capital*), and the *financial capital* of money, tools and markets. When combined, human, financial and social capital create what I call an *economic ecosystem*. Without this foundation, dreams remain just that—dreams.

Once we had the idea for *The Cop-Out*, Colbert and I needed access to a copier and paper (provided after hours by the ILWU union office) and a sympathetic teacher (Burk) to distribute the newspaper. Without those, our ambitions would have gone nowhere, no matter how strong our drive or talent.

Mentors don't just teach us skills like producing a publication; they also help us learn how to develop and maintain economic ecosystems. Without a network of suppliers, customers, distributors and colleagues, the possibilities are limited.

We tend to take this ecosystem for granted, but it all takes money and administration, i.e. *financial and social capital*. The Lanai High basketball team needed a gym, uniforms and basketballs, which were paid for by taxpayers. We also needed a coach, and the taxpayers paid Mr. Matsui's salary as a teacher and his modest stipend as our coach. The taxpayer also paid for our flights to other islands to play in tournaments, which were organized by athletic directors paid by the taxpayers. The players bought their own shoes and incidentals, but the athletics ecosystem took care of everything else.

A Failed Startup

When my sister-in-law E.M.K. and I launched VoltAge magazine in Berkeley, California in pre-World Wide Web 1985, we had no mentors or network; we started from scratch and ended up only producing one issue. The desktop publishing revolution was only months away, but in 1984 the only option was linotype. Lacking experience and a mentor, I decided to buy a used linotype machine rather than pay others to set the type.

Since we each had jobs—she was a travel guide editor I was still running the contracting business in Hawaii—the amount of time and money we could invest in the venture was limited. E.M.K. called distributors and even famous tech entrepreneurs as potential advertisers, but commitments to a new magazine with an uncertain audience are rare. She recruited a writer friend to contribute a column, but other than that, she did everything while all I could do was write two articles.

Even in the Internet age, where thousands of contacts are available online, finding mentors and people willing to help is not guaranteed. Few people are paid to be mentors, and few have surplus energy to invest in people they don't know and new ventures with no track record.

If we'd been funded for a year, we might have slowly assembled a network of distribution, writers, advertisers and contacts willing to promote the magazine, but lacking an economic ecosystem and mentors, we ran out of money and energy after a single issue.

The precursor to the *Mondo 2000* magazine, *High Frontiers*, launched only months before *VoltAge*, and we were ahead of *Wired* magazine by a full eight years (*Wired* launched in1993). If we'd had a network of distributors, advertisers and friends/allies of the magazine, we might have succeeded in launching a path-breaking social-technological publication.

A Success Story

Back in Hawaii at AFSC, one of our projects, the *Peoples Yellow Pages*, provides a good example of how economic ecosystems work. In the pre-Internet 1970s, it was difficult to locate community resources and services. You could find phone numbers in the Yellow Pages, but this was not what we now call a *curated* list of resources. If you didn't know the name of the organization or the correct category, you wouldn't even know it existed.

To get a well-organized, comprehensive list required legwork, and the AFSC decided to assemble and publish a *curated* list of resources as a *socially useful tool* that filled a need few even saw because no such resource had ever been assembled before.

Most of the work was done by volunteers, and the printing costs were paid by donations from AFSC members and supporters. (One of my contributions was to doodle whimsical designs for some of the page numbers; the number 10 became a spoked bicycle wheel, etc.)

Based on users' feedback and wide distribution, the *People's Yellow Pages* successfully expanded the community's access to existing services and resources by putting them all in one easy-to-use guide.

How Economic Ecosystems Function

Examining how a very small AFSC office—one part-time paid staff and a few dedicated volunteers—made this happen helps us understand how economic ecosystems function.

What we notice right away is that while AFSC is small in terms of staff and budget, it is a national organization with international ties, so its network is extensive. While we didn't get much direct support from the national office, we benefited from the organization's sterling reputation and long history of getting hands-on projects done around the world on minimal budgets.

Secondly, AFSC had a structure that was voluntary (what we call *opt-in*) and democratic, but hierarchical in terms of making people accountable to the Area Committee, the organization's management team. Disagreements were settled by a structure of discussion and voting.

Third, membership was a *privilege*, not a *right*. Although it never happened during my years of service, volunteers could be asked to leave. For example, if I'd been rash enough to argue with Colin when he dressed me down for being late, my unsuitability for service would have been self-evident, and I would have been politely but firmly drummed out. For me, arguing with Colin was unthinkable; losing everything I'd worked for in a moment of heated self-justification never entered my mind. In other words, it wasn't a place to *do your own thing* and *demand your rights*; it was a place to listen to your faith and desire to serve. In our self-absorbed consumerist society, this is viewed as a sacrifice, but this sacrifice was absolutely core to one's service and the successful completion of projects. In basketball, the desire to hog the ball must be sacrificed for the good of the team. It's the same principle.

Fourth, as a faith-based organization, volunteers accepted the inevitable petty frictions of human groups, and focused on fellowship and living the Christian ideals of our faith. In non-faith based groups I've encountered, petty squabbles often expanded into the guiding dynamic, and the group became mired in a dysfunctional swamp that eventually dissolved the group in a sea of bad blood.

Fifth, AFSC was self-funded by donations from members and supporters. There were no investors or government funding agency to satisfy.

Sixth, there was a flexible structure for getting projects done. Most of the hands-on *nitty-gritty work* was done by subcommittees of volunteers, with the paid staff (director) assisting as needed. In other words, the organization had a structure to guide operations (the organization of work), and a structure to get the nitty-gritty work done. (I'll discuss operational and nitty-gritty in the next section.)

Compare this wealth of structure, volunteers, network of supporters and funding with the *social capital poverty* of our shoe-string efforts to publish *VoltAge* all on our own, attempting to get all the operational and nitty-gritty work done with no previous experience or mentors to help us. Is it any wonder that *VoltAge* only lasted one issue while the *People's Yellow Pages* continued expanding its reach and value?

No matter how smart, dedicated and principled the people, without an economic ecosystem, overcoming the poverty of tools and social capital is like pushing sand uphill.

Another Example

My experience with the *People's Party of Hawaii* offers another example of the difficulty in assembling an economic ecosystem on the fly, without funding, mentors, tools or a network.

The People's Party was founded on the national level in 1971 to put Benjamin Spock on the presidential ballot as a peace candidate. Rob Hutchinson and a few other volunteers laboriously collected the thousands of signatures of registered voters needed to qualify the People's Party of Hawaii as a legal political party. In early 1974, Rob transferred the Party leadership to my friend Jeff Blair, who then recruited my friend Dexter Cate and me as co-chairs—a shared leadership Jeff called The Triumvirate, much to our amusement. The grandiose Roman title was a real laugh because we had no political power, no money, and no connection to anyone with political power.

Both Jeff and Dexter had a peerless strength of conviction that was not immediately visible to anyone giving them a cursory glance: Jeff was bookish and affable behind his glasses and quiet demeanor, and Dexter could have been dismissed as just another gentle hippie with a full beard and long hair.

I greatly admired Jeff and Dexter for the same reason I was in awe of Colin: they took action in the real world that required great courage to live their principles.

Having concluded that the Selective Service System—the draft—was an unconstitutional infringement of civil liberties, Jeff (who'd attended a military academy as a teen) burned his draft card in front of reporters, and then sometime later went to the Selective Service office with me in tow to do research in their public records.

Duly notified by the staff, the FBI swept in to arrest Jeff, whom I subsequently visited in prison while he awaited bail and legal proceedings. He then defended himself in Federal Court before Judge Martin Pence, who dismissed his claims of unconstitutionality but ended by asking, "Is this the kind of young man we should be sending to prison?" Evidently the judge thought not, as Jeff was freed on a technicality.

Jeff's service on the Triumvirate was interrupted by his return to Caltech (California Institute of Technology) to complete his bachelor's degree. I can't say for certain how many students major in history, biology and economics at Caltech, but Jeff was one of them.

As evidenced by his admittance to elite Caltech and his arguing his own case in federal court, Jeff managed complex regulations with what looked to me like ease. He was the operational brains that kept the People's Party of Hawaii compliant with all the state's requirements. (While I was on the go early as a construction worker and went to sleep early, Jeff was a night owl and would call me around midnight for conversations I only groggily followed.)

Dexter and his wife Suzie had served in the Peace Corps in Sierra Leone (West Africa), and their response to a young man in the village who wanted to become a physician spoke volumes. While the typical response would have been to refer the youth to an official charity, Dexter and Suzie arranged for the young man to enter the U.S. and the University of Hawaii and paid all his expenses until he graduated many years later. During these years, he lived with them in their charmingly dilapidated World war II-era converted Quonset hut home in Manoa Valley.

On top of his job as a school teacher and doing volunteer work for AFSC and the People's Party, Dexter also launched Save the Whales-Hawaii, a non-profit devoted to promoting a global ban on whaling. Dexter had been fascinated by cetaceans since childhood and I remember listening to his recordings of whale communications in his Quonset hut's living room. (I fictionalized Dexter's later heroism in freeing trapped dolphins at night in a raging storm in my novel *For My Daughter*, which I dedicated to his memory.)

While Jeff managed the party's operational requirements, Dexter and I focused on the nitty-gritty of meetings, promoting the party platform, and eventually running Dexter's campaign for Congress. We all had fulltime jobs: I still worked for Island Trends and was finishing my university studies, and Jeff supported himself with an array of quirky jobs such as running the key shop at Sears.

What bound us together was friendship, of course, but also a drive to broaden what we viewed as a narrow, hopelessly corrupted version of elite-dominated democracy that ignored the key issues of the day: sustainability (an issue Colbert and I had promoted in *The Cop-Out* on the first Earth Day in 1970, a watershed moment in the global environmental movement) and entrenched economic and social inequalities.

Political Disillusionment

My two experiences in the conventional political realm had been extremely disappointing. I'd attended a Democratic Party caucus in Manoa with neighbors, a meeting with all the enthusiasm and passion of a Soviet Politburo meeting discussing the collectives' tire production. The same old hacks switched offices in a transparently rigged simulation of actual democracy.

I'd also volunteered a few hours for George McGovern's 1972 presidential campaign. I was ushered into a small office in the Mo'ili'ili district of Honolulu and given a list of phone numbers to call, soliciting support for McGovern on election day. (This was before robo-calling and telemarketing ruined telephone service; back then, if the phone rang, you picked it up, If nobody was home, the phone rang until the caller hung up.)

Was this all that could be done? It seemed to me that the purpose of political activism was to open the *Overton window*, what the general public saw as important and possible, and to introduce ideas and candidates that were truly competitive rather than just the usual reheated leftovers. The

People's Party of Hawaii was the only party which actually addressed the key issues of the era with solutions that weren't facades hiding the same old insiders serving their own interests.

Dexter and Jeff each had a genius for political theater. One of their stunts was to visit the offices of corporations which had donated tens of thousands of dollars to the Democratic and Republican parties, and request an equal donation for the People's Party. To carry the cash, they brought black plastic trash bags adorned with big dollar signs. The corporate leaders declined the request, but it made the point we intended about money and political power—and that got us coverage in the local newspapers.

To emphasize the same point—that money bought political power and corrupted democracy--one of our platform planks was that we would accept no donation that was worth more than a case of beer, which was around $10 at the time.

States make it extremely difficult to start a political party and keep it compliant for the next election, and this goes a long way toward protecting those in power from competing ideas and leadership.

Three individuals with fulltime jobs and other commitments starting from scratch will never be able to compete with established political parties' war chests stuffed with cash, or their paid staff and their ability to dispense political favors to donors. Having ready access to an existing base of potential allies and trusted networks would have enabled the overworked, zero-resources Triumvirate to widen the Overton Window of what was deemed important and politically possible.

Let's pause to summarize what we've gathered so far.

1. People want to belong to something that's purposeful, and they're deprived if they don't have opportunities to belong to something that's meaningful to them.

2. Belonging is an under-appreciated form of wealth. Money can buy stuff, but it can't buy what belonging provides: fulfillment, positive social roles, identity, the dignity of contributing and participation in something larger than oneself.

3. Belonging is a key part of getting ahead, as belonging gives us access to mentors and pathways to productive skills.

4. It is almost impossible to get ahead if you don't have an economic ecosystem.

These raise some obvious questions. Why can't we have a system that guarantees opportunities to belong for everyone? And why can't we have a system that guarantees opportunities to get ahead for everyone?

If we wanted to design such a system, what would it look like?

Operational and Hands-On Mastery

Imagine entering a café with sidewalk tables for lunch. The white-apron-clad waiter welcomes you, and after taking your seat you glance over the counter at the chef and her staff's fast-paced ballet of preparing meals.

While the chef is the natural focus of activity, preparing meals is only part of what it takes to run a restaurant. The other half is managing everything else that's needed to keep the doors open: supervising and scheduling staff, ordering supplies, paying rent, utilities, insurance, etc., managing advertising, meeting with your accountant, paying taxes, arranging a cleaning service, and a hundred other managerial tasks.

The person in the kitchen has to know how to prepare what customers come for--delicious, attractive meals—and do so with a minimum of wasted motion, starting with the prep hours before the first customer is seated. This requires mastery of the *hands-on, nitty-gritty* of cooking for crowds.

But this mastery doesn't automatically translate into *operational* mastery—running the restaurant behind the scenes. The person with the skills to operate such a complex business may not know the first thing about running the kitchen, since these two skillsets are completely different.

Good cooks are accustomed to hearing "you should open a restaurant," as if cooking skills are what matters and everything else will just fall into place. Experienced chefs know that being a good cook is only half of the mastery needed to operate a restaurant—without operational skills, the new restaurant faces a fatal headwind.

Imagine watching a house being built. While the roofers are nailing down shingles, plumbers are installing pipes and carpenters are nailing on siding. The skills each worker needs to complete the tasks are visibly *hands-on*. Less visible are the skills required to organize and manage the onsite choreography: submitting bids, drawing up material lists, conferring with the architect, arranging for building inspections, paying all the bills, overseeing the bookkeeping, scheduling subcontractors and so on in an endless tangle of tasks, each as critical to the construction of the home as the carpenter steadying a board and driving a nail.

The carpenter who knows how to build a house doesn't automatically have the experience to be a general contractor, and the manager running the company might have few hands-on skills: the nitty-gritty skills are completely different from the operational skills.

In observing my bosses Denny and Dan, I learned a few things about being a contractor, but I was woefully unprepared for running such a complex, demanding enterprise despite my hunger to learn. Gaining mastery of operational and nitty-gritty skills takes a long time. Both require learning from seemingly endless mistakes and painful failures. Formal training (Masters of Business Administration, etc.) can provide a structure for this learning, but there's no substitute for real-world experience.

Specialized vs. General Skills

Sometimes we need a bit of both types of skills to get the job done. When my partner Mike and I had built over 40 custom homes for individual clients, we secured the contract to build a 42-unit subdivision. We'd never managed such a big project, and it taxed not just our skills but our ability to withstand extremes of financial and managerial over-reach.

One night a terrific wind and rain storm swept over the island, and I awoke around 2 a.m. wondering if the tarps covering the huge stacks of drywall on the site might have blown loose. If the drywall got soaked, it would be ruined. An MBA with no construction experience might not have thought of this, or assumed that the subcontractor was responsible and so it wasn't an issue. But ultimately, Mike and I were accountable for everything, so I got up, put on a rain coat, drove the two miles to the site and discovered that the tarps were indeed being peeled off by the howling wind. My face lashed by the cold rain, I single-handedly secured all the tarps and went back to bed.

Knowing how to do this can't be put into a YouTube video; there are too many variables: how to get it done depends on the size of the materials being protected, the type of tarps, the availability of heavy wood beams to hold down the tarps, and so on. I don't remember exactly how I secured the tarps because there was nothing memorable about something I'd done many times; the only thing that was memorable was the middle-of-the-night misery.

As if we weren't overwhelmed enough, we won the contract to build a small shopping center, and on the day of the concrete pour, I was walking down the 180-foot length of the newly poured concrete slab when I noticed a wheelchair ramp had been missed; there was a curb where there should have been a ramp. Fortunately the concrete hadn't completely hardened, so I grabbed some tools, cut the curb, dug out the concrete and fashioned the required ramp, more or less in the nick of time. I could have tried to find someone else on the crew and pulled them off what they were doing, but given my 12 years of hands-on experience, it was faster and easier to just do it myself.

The salient point here is that *specialization* is highly rewarded in our economy because the more specialized the worker, the higher their productivity in their field. To maximize profits, the incentives are all in favor of specialized skills. But specialization has its own limitations, and sometimes the greatest value is created by generalists who have a working knowledge of both operational and nitty-gritty skills.

One of the benefits of living in Berkeley, California was the opportunity to dine at the world-famous restaurant Chez Panisse, founded by Alice Waters. Lunch is fairly affordable; the *prix fixe* dinner is pricey. Chez Panisse is famous because it championed what became known as California Cuisine and the farm-to-table collaboration in which local farmers deliver their seasonal produce and the chefs design the day's menu around these fresh ingredients.

Chez Panisse is unique not just for the quality of its cuisine (there are hundreds of other restaurants all over the world serving up *haute cuisine* for a hefty price) but for the global influence of its philosophy of using locally sourced ingredients and preparing them with artful sincerity--simply but with authority, authenticity and an eye on presentation. The effect is intentionally informal rather than fussy.

What's not as widely known is that the restaurant struggled in its early years, and that Water's father provided the financial backing and the managerial expertise needed to get through the first lean years. His operational help was absolutely critical to the success of the restaurant, which went on to be enormously influential in fields ranging from prison gardens to school lunches to *haute cuisine*, as the dozens of chefs and apprentices who learned their craft at Chez Panisse dispersed into the restaurant world.

If Water's father had supported a more conventional restaurant rather than his daughter's, would the other restaurant have had the global influence of Chez Panisse? No, for the simple reason that the Chez Panisse vision was unique to Alice.

In our years in Berkeley, we often hosted large Thanksgiving meals for friends, family and students from around the world who were attending the University of California-Berkeley and were unable to go home for the holiday. One year we were blessed by a friend who was serving an apprenticeship at Chez Panisse, as she brought along two fellow apprentices to help us prepare the feast for two dozen guests from eight countries.

You might think there is not much to be done with mashed potatoes, but these apprentices made mashed potatoes that were a complete revelation to me. I realized that *there is nothing that cannot be improved with mastery*. I also realized that *true wealth is mastery shared*.

Our flat was small, less than 800 square feet, and our kitchen was cramped. We had to combine two households' (our friend's and our own) tables, chairs and dishes to host 23 people, and we used her oven and our propane-fired burner outside to augment our overworked stove.

There were already about six people crammed into our compact kitchen, and the two chefs immediately found a tiny length of counter to start work. One spotted my favorite old Japanese knife, and I was pleased to note she set her own knife aside to use this one.

This chef quickly assembled the sort of fresh greens with accents (pomegranate seeds, etc.) that would grace the cover of a fashionable food magazine, while I apologized to the other chef for asking her to do the lowly tasks of preparing the mashed potatoes and gravy. Rather than be offended by our request, she cheerfully set about making extraordinary mashed potatoes and gravy.

This is true mastery: *no small thing done badly*. This is in keeping with the Chez Panisse philosophy, which aims not for artificial heights of fussiness but artful simplicity and creative use of fresh ingredients.

In the conventional "fancy meal," the mashed potatoes and gravy would be dressed up in some sort of exotica. Here, the chef kept to simple mashed potatoes and gravy, but did so with full mastery.

Both the chefs loved the *Manchurian Gobi* (cauliflower) prepared by our young friends, and my wife's *Buddha's feast*. Mastery is not a brand, nor is it exclusive. Anyone can gain mastery if they're willing to make all the mistakes needed to achieve mastery.

It is only as a participant that one can enjoy freely shared mastery. Someone with a lot of money can sit down and consume a costly meal, but passive consumption can never "taste" mastery, much less understand it as the pure expression of sharing.

I had difficulty sleeping that night, for the experience of participating in preparing the meal was deeply moving. Our young friends had slept over the previous night to help us prepare for the celebration, and afterward the young man told us that he had observed everyone was smiling as they ate. There is no "price tag" on mastery freely shared, on generosity, on caring, on companionship or on friendship and affection, for true wealth is what cannot be bought. You can "buy" servitude but you cannot buy caring, generosity or love.

Wealth measured in money is a cheap facade of meaningless consumption, a threadbare shadow-play put on for others. *Wealth is mastery freely shared.*

The Danger of Over-reach

Once someone reaches a basic operational mastery, the lure of expanding the enterprise beyond their competence arises. I saw the crippling consequences of this over-reach when I went to work for the Owner Builder Center in Berkeley in 1987 as their Communications Coordinator, handling public relations, outreach and the internal newsletter.

Despite the poverty-level pay, for me it was a dream job, as I believed in the mission of this unique non-profit: teaching both hands-on and contracting skills to the general public in evening classes and weekend workshops. Although the need it served might seem obvious, the OBC was the first organization to develop a curriculum of classes and workshops that could be offered by community colleges and other non-profits around the country.

The OBC's founders had developed the right curriculum (portable to other institutions, for a licensing fee) at the right time, as the interest in owner-building and doing home improvement projects was widespread in young home-buyers. (This was pre-YouTube, so video courses on these topics were not yet mainstream.)

The money poured in, and the expansion seemed unstoppable. The founders started a number of projects that stretched finances to the breaking point, such as building a spec house as part of a new Summer Camp program. They'd exceeded their operational expertise by expanding too rapidly and ended up losing control of costs.

By the time I came on board a few years later, the organization was struggling to stay afloat. The office was littered with big, costly copying machines that had been leased from vendors and then abandoned; private loans solicited from Berkeley residents had gone unpaid, and even the teachers—contractors who taught in the evenings or weekends—had been stiffed and were getting back pay in sporadic dribbles. The extensive course catalog was halfway between a magazine and a catalog, as expensive as a magazine to produce but without the advertising revenues. The staff included numerous part-timers with ill-defined jobs and a Program Director with little experience; her parents were major creditors, and so the job had gone to her.

Accountability was poor, and criticism of past decisions was defensively dismissed as "the blame game." Management was an ungainly stew of a Board of Directors, a Management Team and a Teachers Advisory Committee. Everyone that we now call *stakeholders* had a say, but there was no agreed-upon process for making decisions, especially painful decisions to cut staffing and expenses, a necessity if we were to save the ship from sinking.

Eventually, the necessary cuts were made: we moved to a much less expensive and more useful space, part-time staff was let go, managerial complexity was reduced, the course catalog lost the costly ambition to be a magazine, and we added new courses for the first time in years, expanding revenues and our public visibility. The financial swamp was slowly drained as we paid the teachers' back pay, and we capped the renewal with a 10th anniversary party attended by the city's mayor and local media.

The lessons were numerous: a group can have admirable ambition and talent, but if it doesn't have an appropriate structure and operational skills, even the best ideas and organizations can founder. The OBC prospered for a few years but was eventually sunk by the recession of 1990-1991, which caused enrollment to plummet.

Several of us launched a follow-on non-profit, the Building Education Center, which served the community until 2012 when key staffers retired. (I'd resigned a decade earlier when I realized there was nothing more I could contribute.)

All these experiences raised a question in my mind: why couldn't we have a system that offered operational and hands-on resources to every organization, no matter how new or small?

Workarounds and Reinventing Ourselves

The conventional path to success is well-worn: get a degree from an elite university, go to work for an elite company, rise up to an elite position in the company, and then from that great height, move up whatever ladder you choose in the public or private sector. All of this is easier if you *choose your parents wisely*, i.e. get born into a wealthy family with insider connections.

The conventional path to home ownership is equally straightforward: get a secure, well-paying job, maintain good credit while you save up a down payment, buy the house with a mortgage and then spend the next 30 years paying it off.

There are unconventional alternatives, and since they are contingent on specifics, we call them *workarounds*. They're not as clear-cut as the conventional path because each workaround depends on the situation and the individuals.

For me, the workaround was to (1) learn how to build a house myself, other than a few other trades that required licensed subcontractors; (2) save up as much money as possible by living extremely frugally, and start building with that cash, and (3) make money doing small construction jobs on the side to raise more cash while I worked on my house.

As you'll discover in the section on money, I eventually borrowed some money from the bank as a personal loan to finish the house, but I paid this loan off in a year or two.

This patchwork solution isn't for everyone, of course, but it worked for me and many other tradespeople.

The point here is that if the conventional path is blocked, the typical advice is to give up, as if the conventional path is the only path. But it isn't the only way forward. There are workarounds that reach the desired goal but in an unconventional and often creative fashion.

When Steve Jobs set the goal of designing the Macintosh computer, he didn't want to lose control of the project to the formidable Apple bureaucracy, and so he isolated the team in a separate building and pushed the project with tyrannical energy. It took Jobs' unique intensity and creativity to make this workaround pay off.

The conventional path to a career is to go to college and get a diploma. How much you actually learned is an unknown to future employers, but the conventional view is that persevering to get the degree *signals* your worthiness to potential employers.

As I explained in my book *Get a Job, Build a Real Career and Defy a Bewildering Economy*, this signal is inherently weak, and so employers are increasingly demanding real work experience and accomplishments—exactly what credentials don't document. Many employers are realizing that college diplomas are not accurate reflections of employees' skills or productivity.

Since our economy rewards specialization because it increases productivity and profits, adding specialized skills via additional college diplomas is the conventional path to higher pay.

But in many fields this path is now crowded, and those holding newly minted Master's Degrees and PhDs are finding there are far more people with these diplomas than there are jobs that require them.

The workaround I've lived by, and outlined in my book *Get a Job*, is a process I call *accredit yourself*. Rather than rely on the weak signal of an accredited institution issuing a diploma that doesn't reflect the students' knowledge, skills and *human/social capital*—their emotional intelligence and ability to work effectively with others—it's faster, better and cheaper to *accredit yourself* by mastering real-world skills via on-the-job experience and then documenting your accomplishments.

Accrediting yourself follows the dictum of American philosopher Ralph Waldo Emerson: *Do the thing and you shall have the power.* In other words, start doing what you want to learn, and eventually you'll gain the power of mastery.

My longtime friend G.F.B. (my only friend from my year at Punahou), who inspired me to write this book, has gently poked fun at me for repeatedly jumping into a field I know nothing about, and somehow ending up with some sort of expertise. This is the workaround to mastery: *Do the thing and you shall have the power.*

When someone moves into a field that's new to them, or begins anew after a crushing defeat, we say they're *reinventing themselves.* The process of reinventing may look random, but it's actually connecting the dots to build on everything you've assembled: failures, skills, connections and economic ecosystems.

We reinvent ourselves for many reasons: we reach the end of one career and need to move on; we want to fulfill a long-held ambition that's been set aside for years; we feel stifled in a dead-end job, or we've suffered a major setback: been laid off, our business failed, a personal crisis caused us to burn out, etc.

For me, leaving the building industry to pursue a writing career was all these things: I'd already done everything I'd hoped to accomplish as a builder, and so every future project would be repeating what I'd already done. The immense stresses of co-managing all our projects had burned me out emotionally, financially and physically; my mental health was shattered. Mike and I had barely kept the business afloat as the soaring material and labor costs of the multi-million dollar subdivision had eaten us alive.

At the time, it seemed to me I had no skills other than building, and so I felt I was truly starting over at age 33. My degree in philosophy had no market value, nor did it give me any marketable skills. I was at low ebb, and since a career as a writer seemed beyond farfetched, I forced myself to consider other fields: I made an appointment with the dean of the school of Architecture at my alma mater, U.H.-Manoa, and he very generously described the three years of coursework I'd need to get a diploma.

Though my musical ability was on par with my athletic skills---below average—I even considered the precarious field of live music as a possibility.

Testing one's interest in a field is useful, as it leads one to realize that either this is something I have the boundless enthusiasm needed to achieve mastery or it's something that is best left as a hobby.

I was clueless about two important things. One was expressed by *Wired* magazine co-founder Kevin Kelly: "Following your bliss is a recipe for paralysis if you don't know what you are passionate about. A better motto for most youth is 'master something, anything'. Through mastery of one thing, you can drift towards extensions of that mastery that bring you more joy, and eventually discover where your bliss is."

In other words, if you master one thing, you've also learned something extremely valuable about the process of gaining mastery, a process you can apply to another field.

The second thing I didn't understand was the dot-connecting described by Steve Jobs: *our experiences can connect in ways we didn't anticipate or plan.* As Jobs explained, how the dots eventually connect is only visible in hindsight, but that doesn't mean we can't make an effort in the present to understand how we might advance based on the experiential wealth of our human and social capital, even if we feel like we've suffered a crushing setback.

Burned out and at the lowest point of my adult life, I had enough sense to get some help, and I turned to psychiatrist Mary DeLuca for counseling. She helped me realize that I was focusing all my attention on my failures to the exclusion of what I'd accomplished. Even if the building business had been a financial failure, hadn't we paid everyone? Hadn't we given people gainful employment? Hadn't we built numerous houses for homeowners? Hadn't I learned something valuable?

Looking back, what Dr. DeLuca was trying to get me to appreciate was the *human and social capital* I'd gained in the crazy-busy years of building and the brief foray into magazine publishing (*VoltAge*). At the time I berated myself for not taking a safe, low-risk job without all the crushing stress. Looking back, it's clear I had no enthusiasm for a safe job because there was no way to fulfil my ambitions on that path.

Though I didn't understand it at the time, I now understand that failure and struggling to learn difficult things is when we learn the most. To say "I don't want to struggle or fail" is to say "I don't want to learn fast and gain mastery."

Workarounds are inherently risky and difficult because the path isn't paved like the conventional road. Many times, we have to slash our own path through a seemingly impenetrable jungle. As a result, mistakes and failures are part of any workaround, just as they're part of reinventing yourself.

Though I really didn't understand my *human and social capital*, I reckoned my experience in building might give me an entry to the field I was trying to break into, writing. The part-time, low-pay job at OBC was the first such step, and that led to a chance to meet the editor of the *San Francisco Examiner's* home and garden section, Bruce Koon, who gave me my first freelance writing assignments. Over time, this led to feature stories and the chance to write dozens of articles and columns for the *Examiner*, the *San Francisco Chronicle*, the *San Jose Mercury-News* and many other publications.

The conventional path to this career was to get a college degree in journalism. Since I didn't have that, nor the time, money or enthusiasm to get another degree, I had to pursue the workaround of freelancing to reinvent myself as an independent writer-journalist.

At the same time, I decided to finish my first novel and seek a literary agent. Again, the conventional path to being a novelist is to get a college degree in literature and creative writing. Lacking this, I was left with Emerson's dictum and little else. I didn't find a mentor for either journalistic writing or fiction, and so I felt my way forward one step at a time.

I hadn't completely abandoned my interest in philosophy, so I took a paper I wrote on one of my interests, artificial intelligence (AI), to the philosophy department at University of California-Berkeley, where I'd audited several classes. I was told getting admitted to the graduate program was a longshot at best, and once again I had to assess whether my enthusiasm was sufficient to fuel a five-year program with zero funding. I realized my interest in AI would have to remain an informal hobby rather than the paved path to a graduate degree.

I think you see a pattern here: like most people, I kept trying to connect the dots of my enthusiasms with conventional pathways and finding it simply didn't work for me.

Since conventional paths were too costly, time-consuming and specialized, the only alternative was to continue slashing my way through the jungle by reinventing myself.

Looking back now, I can connect the dots in ways I didn't see at the time: my experiences with *The Cop-Out*, *VoltAge* and free-lance writing provided the foundations I would need to manage my blog and book-writing careers; my founding and managing a complicated construction company gave me an unparalleled understanding of how the economy functions in the real world, and experiences with AFSC, the People's Party of Hawaii and the Owner

Builder Center enabled me to understand the challenges and difficulties of managing organizations. In each case, I was learning through workarounds and reinventing myself, a process that connects the dots of our experience, often without our even seeing the connections snapping together.

It would have been helpful if I'd had some kind of supportive ecosystem to help me understand and manage these uncertain processes. Why wasn't there some kind of organization I could belong to that actually encouraged workarounds and reinventing ourselves?

Even genius has difficulty with the process of reinventing ourselves. Steve Jobs hit his own low point after he was fired from Apple, and in his biography (written by Walter Isaacson) he confessed to fearing that he would be remembered more as a failure than as an innovator. Jobs' habit throughout his life was to take long walks, often with a close friend, and work out ideas on those leisurely walks.

After a period of such soul-searching, Jobs launched a new computer company, NeXT, that was eventually sold to Apple for the value of its operating system around the time he returned to save Apple from what appeared to be certain bankruptcy. In his years outside Apple, Jobs also acquired Pixar Animation from *Star Wars* director-producer George Lucas, launching Pixar's rocket to animation glory.

Few of us have the genius and drive to operate on such a global scale, but the point here is even Steve Jobs got fired, felt lost and had to find a way to reinvent himself. From the luxury of the present, we can look back at his extraordinary career and say it was destined, but if Jobs had been unable to connect the dots between his human/social/financial capital and his enthusiasms, he may well have faded into relative obscurity as an eccentric who soared to the heights with Apple and then crashed back to earth.

We've already asked: what if there was an organization everyone could belong to that offered every individual gainful employment, not just for profitable work but for socially valuable work? What if this organization also provided a means for every member to access mentors who could help them gain mastery of productive skills? And what if this organization encouraged workarounds and reinventing ourselves as pathways to *getting ahead*?

What would such an organization look like? How would it be structured? How would it work operationally and on the nitty-gritty level?

In Times of Transition, Adaptability and Flexibility are Wealth

In reviewing my recurring interest in the conventional path of going back to college for another degree, you've probably noticed the same thing that struck me: the conventional path is so time-consuming and costly that if I'd pursued a credential for all my interests, I'd be an old, poor man before I got through all the programs.

In other words, if you won't be happy spending your entire life in one specialty, then you're more or less forced to pursue workarounds and reinvention because these are the only practical ways to get ahead.

They have another advantage: workarounds and reinvention are far more adaptable and flexible than conventional paths. They can be modified on the fly, or dropped in favor of a superior path. The conventional paths are rigid— no diploma for you if you're one class shy of the requirement—and they have significant *sunk costs*, meaning that the investment required is so large that we can't change course mid-stream without losing everything we've invested—very likely years of our life and thousands of dollars. And so we stick with a program that will only cause us future dissatisfaction because we can't bear losing everything we've invested in it.

There are many problems with rigid, time-consuming, costly pathways. The first is incorrectly assessing our enthusiasm for the field. Maybe our initial enthusiasm fades as we learn more about the field, or maybe we were more enthused about the potential for high pay than the actual work.

The second is that our initial assessment of the market for our new credential may be way off-base by the time we graduate, and there are few job openings and too many graduates with the same credential—a classic supply-demand imbalance.

The third is that the field has changed so rapidly that very little of what we learned in the conventional program applies to the real world.

These three problems are common in eras of rapid transition. History shows that economic and social orders are generally stable for long periods of time where not much changes. But these long stretches of stability are inevitably interrupted by eras of rapid, tumultuous changes. These eras of transition have many causes: wars, revolutions, pandemics, famines, ecological disasters, religious movements and technological-social innovations that disrupt the Old Order. (In science, this pattern of stability being interrupted by periods of rapid evolution is known as *punctuated equilibrium*.)

In the past few hundred years, these periods of rapid, dramatic change include: the transition from most people working in agriculture to mass employment in industry, from monarchy to democracy, from industrial to post-industrial, from analog to digital, and from an economy producing goods to an economy of services.

We are in a highly disruptive and unpredictable transition from a highly centralized, oil/credit-based consumer economy destabilized by enormous wealth inequality and *pay-to-play* democracy, to a decentralized, digital de-growth economy focused on social value and sustainability rather than corporate profits.

As I noted in the Introduction, the entrenched Old Guard that has gotten rich in the old order will fight with everything they have to stop the tides from sweeping away their feeding trough. This self-serving resistance won't stop the forces of history, but it will resist any reform.

As a result, change will come from workarounds that obsolete the old order, not from the incremental reforms that typify periods of stability.

Given all the conflicting forces at work in eras of rapid transition, it's easy to get overwhelmed by the complexity of it all. But fortunately for us, beneath all the surface complexity, systems share simple dynamics that help us understand what's going on amidst all the noise and chaos.

I'll discuss my interest in systems in the next section, but for the present discussion, we'll focus on two dynamics that differentiate systems in stable eras and those that are in transitional periods.

Author Nassim Taleb's book *Anti-Fragile* explains that systems can be either fragile or robust—what he calls "anti-fragile"—depending on how they're structured. Anti-fragile systems actually get stronger when they're buffeted by volatility, while fragile systems collapse.

Highly centralized, interconnected systems are *tightly bound*. One way to visualize a tightly bound system is to imagine intersecting circles of dominoes like the Olympic logo. If one domino in one circle falls, it will topple every domino in every circle. This is a very fragile system, because any domino falling can end up toppling the whole thing. This is how a relatively limited financial crisis in American subprime mortgages in 2008 almost took down the entire global financial system.

Another key dynamic is that systems which look *linear* can suddenly become *non-linear*. Snow falling on a mountainside is linear, meaning that every inch of snow that falls adds about an inch to the snow piling up on the mountainside: one inch of cause has one inch of effect. (In the language of systems, we say the falling snow is an *input* and the rising snow depth is an *output*.) When another inch of snow added to the snowpack triggers an avalanche, that's non-linear, as the *input* (one more inch of snow) triggered a much larger *output*/effect: the entire snowpack roars down the mountainside, destroying everything in its path.

Another way to visualize linear/non-linear is to imagine setting up two dominoes close together. If one falls, it will only topple one other domino. That's a linear system: one domino topples one domino.

Now imagine five intersecting rings of dominoes where a single domino topples all the dominoes in the entire system when it falls. That's non-linear.

In periods of transition, all the dominoes in fragile, centralized systems can be toppled by seemingly small changes.

Since 2008, the extremes required to keep the system glued together that I described in my book *Why Our Status Quo Failed and Is Beyond Reform* have only increased the fragility of our economic and social systems.

We need to understand one more concept to grasp why adaptability and flexibility are so valuable in times of transition: *optimization*. When we optimize something, we're aiming to get the most bang for our buck: maximize our efficiency, profit, productivity, etc., while minimizing our costs. How we optimize something depends on what we choose to optimize.

For example, if we want to assemble as many autos as possible in a day, we'd choose an assembly line production. But if we want to optimize quality control so each car has the fewest possible defects, then we might choose a team-assembly process, where a team assembles one entire car at a time.

There are always trade-offs in optimization, because we can't optimize everything. If we optimize the number of autos assembled, we have to accept a higher defect rate. If we optimize quality control, we have to accept a lower number of autos assembled, but they will have fewer defects.

In the decades-long economic expansion after World War II, employers got the most bang for the buck by hiring workers with training from trade schools or college, and then having those workers stay in the same field their entire careers. In this *factory-model* economy, a *factory-model* educational system of centralized campuses and standardized curriculum optimized the mass production of millions of trained workers. This system optimized productivity in large, stable organizations such as corporations and government agencies. It was common for people to work for the same company or agency their whole lives, as the organizations' products and processes didn't change much. The era was so stable that companies could invest in worker training and be confident their investment would pay off, because the entire process was stable and therefore predictable.

All these optimizations no longer work because everything is changing rapidly and in unpredictable ways. As products and processes become obsolete, *factory-model* training no longer prepares students for real-world work. Which skills companies will need is difficult to predict, so there is an over-supply of graduates with credentials of questionable value, as the diploma itself doesn't give potential employers much information about what the graduate actually knows and what skills they will bring to the job.

In the post-war expansion, a college diploma in any field had a high value because the diploma signaled to employers that the graduate had successfully completed the factory-model education that prepared them for a career in a conventional organization.

But in today's tumultuous transition, diplomas outside of specific professional careers such as nurse or physician have an uncertain value. In this era, what's valuable is being flexible and adaptable and having a wide range of operational and social skills that can be applied in all sorts of fields.

What does being adaptable and flexible mean? It means being willing to learn new things and work in new ways. Put another way, it means being comfortable finding workarounds and reinventing yourself.

We're so accustomed to measuring wealth solely in terms of money that we overlook what's truly valuable: belonging and being adaptable/flexible.

What Does It Mean to 'Get Ahead'?

Now that we've reached the end of the section, you may be thinking, what exactly does *getting ahead* mean?

Getting ahead means you have opportunities to belong to something purposeful that's meaningful to you, something that offers you gainful employment, i.e. a chance to contribute that provides a reliable paycheck while advancing your career as well as the goals of the organization.

Getting ahead means having opportunities to achieve mastery of operational and hands-on skills (human capital) and build social and financial capital.

In other words, getting ahead means accumulating forms of wealth that can't be measured in money: belonging to an organization that values your contributions and offers opportunities to build all the forms of the wealth that can't be taken from you: operational, hands-on and social skills, adaptability/flexibility, and the ability to reinvent yourself.

More specifically, getting ahead means having a position in an organization (or economic ecosystem) that has the following eight characteristics:

1. The individual and the job are well-matched in terms of personality, skills and goals.
2. The workload is manageable and sustainable.

3. Everyone has some control of their work, a choice of tasks and responsibilities, and a say in group decisions.
4. Everyone earns rewards and recognition commensurate with their effort and expertise.
5. The community/workgroup values everyone's efforts and contributions, and trusts/supports each member.
6. Everyone is treated fairly and equally.
7. The work environment and purpose aligns with the individual's values.
8. A position that enables self-expression, fulfillment of ambitions and interests, with a path to higher skills and responsibilities or into new fields of endeavor.

The greater the number of these that are present, the greater our sense that we're *getting ahead*. The fewer of these that are present, the keener our sense of getting nowhere or falling behind. If all eight are impaired, these deficiencies grease the slide into failure for both the individual and the organization.

Gaining Agency

There is one more important component of getting ahead: gaining control over one's life, and power over one's circumstances. The fancy word for this is *agency*. To have agency is to control one's circumstances. To have agency, one must accept responsibility, what many now call *ownership*, of one's choices, labor and skills. Rather than being helplessly swept along by river currents, individuals with agency grab the oars and steer toward their own personal destination.

When you're desperate for work because you need the money, you overlook all the warning signs that things could turn out badly.

Here's my own personal example of this:

Shortly after securing the loan to finish my first building project, I set out to find some paying work so I could make the loan payments. Due to fast-rising inflation, interest rates were shooting higher, strangling the interest-sensitive sectors of auto sales and housing. There just wasn't much building going on, and I came up empty after visiting every house under construction in town.

I got a job offer from a contractor who had *fly-by-night* written all over him. He had no office or regular crew, and had a .32 automatic in his briefcase; if everything is on the up and up, why would this guy need a pistol in his briefcase? He had a contract for a two-story house, and he offered me a lump-sum payment for hanging the drywall and doing the finish carpentry—installing the doors, trim and cabinetry. With no other prospects, I swallowed my doubts and took the subcontracting job.

Although the contractor claimed he'd submitted my invoices for payment by the bonding company—the lumber yard that disbursed the funds from the bank as construction proceeded—I never got a payment, and Mr. Fly-by-Night disconnected his phone and flew the coop.

Stiffed for a month's labor, I vowed to escape the powerlessness of being dependent on others for work—and for fair payment. I decided to get my general contractor's license so I could bid on projects and have some control over my work and income. In other words, I decided to acquire *agency*—ownership of my work and circumstances.

Agency is rarely free. It takes enormous effort to choose a destination and row toward it, especially if the currents are fighting you. In my case, gaining ownership required starting a business and getting everything that was required to obtain the license: renting an office in a commercial area, paying for liability, disability and workers compensation insurance, and posting a bond to guarantee any projects I abandoned would be completed. I also had to open up accounts to pay estimated federal and state taxes.

None of this effort and expense guaranteed me a single dollar of income; it was all a costly, time-consuming gamble that I could find people who wanted me to build their house even as the economy slid into recession.

It was a crazy bet, far too risky given the poor economic backdrop and my inexperience in handling the financial pressures as the contractor who had to front the money to get the project to the point where a partial payment would be released by the bank. But since I'd tasted the bitter fruits of powerlessness, I was willing to accept the risks to gain agency.

There is always risk in trying something new and taking responsibility for one's life. But not everyone who wants ownership/agency can afford to take such risks - and getting ahead shouldn't require such enormous gambles.

As a result, it's apparent that one major requirement of our alternative system is that it must be easy for every member to gain agency without betting the farm. All members should be able quit a project in favor of another one, or start their own project with a minimum of effort and zero money.

Section Four:
Understanding Systems

My Fascination with Systems

Although they've practically disappeared from daily life, hand-written letters can hold extraordinary revelations.

It was a typical get-together with my longtime friend, Jim Erler, visiting his 93-year old father in an assisted-living facility in Palo Alto, California. As we were heading down to the dining hall for dinner, Jim mentioned that he'd come across a letter in his father's papers that his Mom had written to her mother. One section dealt with her first impressions of me based on the conversation Jim and I had in the back seat on a multi-hour drive up to their cabin in Big Bear Lake, California. Jim and I had first met and become friends in the 6th grade, when I was 12 and he was 13, and so Jim's Mom was writing about the interests of two young boys.

Though I don't recall the conversation, it seemed Jim and I were talking about religion and science, two subjects of keen interest to me then and now. Based on what she overheard, Jim's Mom described me rather extravagantly as a "genius."

I think what she meant was *precocious*, when a child has an interest or talent far beyond what is typical for their age. I imagine we've all witnessed children with adult-level interests. My young friend Katharine K. had an artistic ability as a child that exceeded every adult I knew with a graduate degree in fine arts. Her sense of proportion, color, detail and design is dazzling to anyone who has tried their hand at painting or drawing. Her creativity is spontaneous; while the person with average talent would struggle to create a handful of brilliant designs, Katharine does so seemingly without effort.

When I recounted the shock I felt when Jim read his Mom's letter aloud, Jim's response was thought-provoking: *"How would your life had been different if you'd read this letter when you were 12"*? In other words, how would knowing that a well-educated and sophisticated adult recognized some special potential in me have changed my view of myself and my prospects? What decisions might I have made if I'd had this extraordinary boost?

I couldn't help feeling that my life would have been different if I'd read the letter at 12 rather than at 60.

What made the letter especially striking is my own parents had never given me any sense that I was anything more than a well-behaved, average boy. It seems parents who recognize their own children's talents are rare; Jim's Mom was effusive about my precociousness but silent about her own son's remarkable abilities in music. I can still remember my amazement at the technical mastery of Jim's own piano compositions at the age of 13. What might have been different in Jim's life if a worldly adult had recognized his musical interests and abilities?

The letter made me realize that my interest in systems, both in the external world of science and the internal world of experience, was innate. I was born to be fascinated by the planets, the structure of atoms, and the mysteries of quasars. I was equally interested in systems we experience that are invisible to others. Rituals, sermons and services did not move me. What drew me was the inner experiences of contemplation, belief and insight.

As a teen I realized a career in the sciences was a poor fit for my mediocre ability in math and my wide-ranging interests; I could never be happy in a narrow field, regardless of the field, and I was in too much of a hurry to spend the decade or more needed to obtain college diplomas in more than one field. And who would hire a generalist with a mixed bag of unconnected credentials when narrow expertise is what's sought after?

After further thought, I'm not so sure that reading the letter would have changed much in my life because there's simply no market for what Jim's Mom saw in me. People with a knack for art, music, theology / philosophy, etc., or an eclectic mix of interests have two choices: they can follow the conventional path and become teachers or scholars in art, music, etc., or they can try to commercialize their art, music, ideas, etc.

Since the market for art, music, ideas, etc. is small, as a general rule those who succeed in commercializing their work also have an innate knack for self-promotion and marketing, as well as enormous appetites for risk (i.e. remaining poor and unknown despite years of hard work). Being able to persevere despite a dispiriting lack of success is also essential.

But even with all these tools in hand, most will fail to commercialize their work because the markets are so small and the competition so keen. When we look at the pathways taken by famous musicians, composers, artists and thinkers, we're guilty of *survivor bias*: we're only seeing the few who reached the pinnacle of fame and fortune, not the thousands who failed despite their talent and drive.

We also aren't seeing the hundreds of others with equal talent who gave up because they couldn't bear the burdens of failure, disappointment and self-doubt and were not adept at self-promotion and marketing. Others gave up their dreams because poverty and overwork ground them down. Some few persevered because *they had no other choice but to continue*, but this didn't guarantee success; their canvases, compositions and manuscripts were unceremoniously dumped in the trash once they passed away.

A select few were able to commercialize their talents in conventional fields—composing music for TV series, for example—or taking their knack for art and commercializing it in much larger markets such as industrial design. This ability to find a market for one's talent is itself a knack that relatively few have.

As foolish as this sounds, I think the only job that would have suited me was to be paid to research and write about whatever interested me, and there are no such jobs. But strangely enough, with the emergence of the World Wide Web and blogs, the dots in my life experience connected so that I eventually ended up being paid by readers to write about whatever interested me—including the systems that have fascinated me since childhood.

In the context of exploring workarounds to conventional systems, the question all this raises is: could we design an alternative system that enables people to find a livelihood that engages their innate talents? I don't mean getting paid to do whatever you want; I mean gainful employment that matches each individual's interests and ambitions in some fashion, while encouraging individuals' other interests as *side projects* within the system.

The key idea here is that the alternative system recognizes the importance to the individual and the community of pursuing interests that may not have obvious markets.

In the conventional system, tinkerers and thinkers who come up with something marketable that generates millions of dollars in sales are lauded, and every other tinkerer and thinker is ignored because whatever they're doing has no value: after all, if it had any marketable value, it would be racking up sales and profits.

The reason why the community at large would benefit from individuals *pursuing interests that may not have obvious markets* as unpaid side projects is that their work might have *social value that has no financial value*. Even if it has no apparent market value, if the pursuit gives meaning and fulfillment to the tinkerer/creator, then that individual becomes a happier, more productive person in whatever work they're doing that does serve the community.

Nature is wasteful in this way. Just as plants generate an immense surplus of seeds, far more than are needed to propagate the species, humans generate a surplus of creativity. Just as the surplus seeds feed other species and support the ecosystem, human creativity feeds both the creators' need to create and the economic ecosystem they inhabit. And just as relatively few seeds actually sprout and reach maturity, relatively few ideas become marketable.

Natural selection revels in variety and surpluses. The greater the variety, the greater the potential for cross-pollination and the emergence of new forms of value. Even if some creative idea has no apparent value at the moment, it may develop value later in different circumstances.

A system that only assigns value to whatever generates profitable sales is impoverished by its narrow definition of value, and the people in that system who have few outlets for their creativity are equally impoverished.

For these reasons, the alternative system must encourage and support members' side projects, not with a paycheck but with an ecosystem that enables cross-pollination, innovation and authentic expression even when there is no immediate market value to the work.

External and Internal Systems

You've probably noticed that I've discussed economic (i.e. external) systems and our experience (i.e. internal) living within these systems. These internal experiences are largely ignored by economics, which naively assumes all humans need to be happy is enough money to consume more today than they did yesterday.

As we saw with the example of paying the lonely kid to shoot baskets by himself, buying stuff is no substitute for what humans truly need: to belong, to get ahead, to fulfill our talents, to earn dignity and self-respect and be part of something greater than ourselves.

In my view, this means we need to design our system to produce not just stuff to consume but also the intangible (yet very real) forms of value: belonging, positive social roles, human and social capital, fulfillment of innate talents and pathways to getting ahead. We are not just robots borrowing and spending money in an economy that only measures consumption and profits. We are human beings with complex social and individual needs.

Early Searches for Systemic Understanding: Marxism, Buddhism and Taoism

Before the formal study of systems (*systems analysis*) arose in the 20th century, the search for systemic understanding was the purview of natural science, theology and philosophy. In my university studies in philosophy, I was introduced to three very different systems that were completely new to me: Marxism, Buddhism and Taoism.

Marxism

Routinely dismissed in America as a failure due to its association with Communism, Marx's work was an attempt to bring scientific rigor to two big ideas. One was Hegel's notion that history isn't just a random jumble of human cruelties and natural disasters, it was *teleological*, meaning it had a trajectory toward a better world. Another was that capital had built-in advantages over labor, and so capital could exploit labor rather than the other way around.

Marx's work focused on the narratives of history and social-economic inequalities, though it has a moral foundation few explore. Rather than accept that "this is the way it's always been and the way it always will be," Marx started from the view that exploitation of labor was wrong. Rather than couch this in moral terms, Marx saw the dominance of capital—i.e. capitalism—as the current stage of human development that was soon to be replaced by a better system that wasn't based on exploitation.

Marx saw social and economic dynamics as one system. The economic system alienated workers from the fruits of their labor, and *melts all that is solid into air*, meaning the economic dominance of capital dissolved social roles, the glue that holds human societies together. Capitalism disrupts social stability not as a goal but as an inevitable consequence of capital's single-minded obsession with maximizing profits.

In other words, Marx wasn't writing only about abstract economics; he was interested in the disruptive consequences of economic systems on society, and in the individual's experience of work and ownership (or non-ownership) of that work.

Marx described many of the economic dynamics we are witnessing today: the stagnation of wages and the expansion of global production to the point that there were more goods and services than workers could afford to buy, so that producers could no longer make a profit except by financial engineering. One example of this is when auto manufacturers make more money from auto loans than from actually making cars. He also described the forces within capitalism that lead to monopolies and cartels. Since these are the most reliably profitable forms of capital, they have the wealth to buy political influence to protect their lock on markets.

Where Marx stumbled was on his vision of history's next stage, Communism. Unlike his analysis of capitalism, his descriptions of the next stage were little more than hazy, idealized sketches. Perhaps he reckoned that since this higher stage of human development was inevitable, there was no need to spend much time on it.

I was fortunate to have an energetic young professor, Fred Bender, who'd compiled a volume of Marx's early writings, and he was able to explain concepts that were lost in the thicket of Marx's dense prose.

Buddhism

My course in Buddhism was taught by an eminent scholar, Professor David Kalupahana, who was very approachable even by us lowly undergrads. Once when my friend G.F.B. and I went to his office to discuss a doctrine he'd outlined in class, an earthquake shook the building. "You see," he said as soon as the temblor stopped. "As the Buddha taught, everything can change in a minute."

Buddhism is an *internal system* of moral and spiritual cultivation leading to the cessation of all desire and an all-encompassing understanding of the nature of existence known as *Enlightenment*. The individual pursues this cultivation by following the *Eight-Fold Path*, guidelines to moral and spiritual attainment and liberation.

The Buddha's precepts did not deal with economic or political policies; instead they were entirely internal to the practitioner. The Buddha presented his doctrines as straightforward cause-and-effect (*The Four Noble Truths*): thoughts and actions generate effects. How we control our thoughts and actions will alter the effects of our thoughts and actions. In other words, our thoughts alter our emotions and our actions, so controlling our thoughts is the key to gaining insight and living a spiritually rewarding life.

Taoism

My courses in Taoism were taught by Professor Chang Chung-yuan (1907-1988), whom I would occasionally see doing Tai Chi late at night on his front yard in Manoa Valley, which happened to be a few doors down from the Quaker Meeting House and AFSC. Professor Chang was 66 at the time, and to my youthful gaze he looked like a Taoist sage in a modern Chinese tunic: graying hair, an august presence, a man of few words but intensely interested in communicating the mysteries of Taoism. (He was awarded a teaching prize by the university a few years after I graduated.)

One of the most famous lines in the Taoist classic the *Tao Te Ching* by Laozi (Lao Tzu) is the first line: "The Tao that can be spoken of is not the Tao itself." (This is Professor Chang's translation of the Chinese text.) One clever student in the class reckoned this meant there was nothing that could be written about the Tao, either, and so he handed in a brief two-paragraph essay for his term paper. Professor Chang's indignant response was as close to outrage as he was capable of: "Even Lao Tzu managed to write 5,000 characters about the Tao!"

Taoism is a mystical philosophy of paradoxes and metaphors that apply to both the external world of politics and society, and the inner world of insight, tranquility and spiritual mastery. The other classic of Taoism *Chuang Tzu* (by Zhuangzi), offers many stories of physical mastery that exemplify the Taoist ideal of effortless action (*wu wei*) which can only be acquired by rigorous practice and self-discipline.

As for the Taoist principles for political and social order, consider Chapter 58 of the *Tao Te Ching* (again, Professor Chang's translation, published in 1975):

When the country is governed through simplicity and leniency,

The people are genuine and honest.

When the country is governed through harshness and sharp investigation,

The people are more deceitful and dishonest.

Taoism describes universal dynamics that govern the entire world of Nature and human life. For example, Professor Chang—who would often write Chinese characters on the blackboard with energetic intensity to make a point—rendered the first line in Chapter 40 as *Reverse is the movement of Tao*. (Others have translated it as *Reversal is the movement of Tao*. My interpretation is: *The way of the Tao is reversal*.)

Given the ambiguity of Taoist concepts, this line has many interpretations. The way of the Tao is reversal because the Tao is fundamentally about virtue, power and what we might call authenticity. Thus all that is falsely presented as permanent will be revealed as impermanent, all that is falsely presented as true will be revealed as false and all that is falsely presented as virtuous will be revealed as fraud.

In terms of systems, Taoism might be considered a "system of no system," as it offers neither guidelines nor a tidy narrative, but one lesson is clear: those who govern least govern best. Those who try to tightly control everything to benefit their own greed for status, wealth and power end up losing everything, a dynamic described in Chapter 9 of the *Tao Te Ching*:

To hold things and to be proud of them is not as good as not to have them,

Because if one insists on an extreme, that extreme will not dwell long.

When a room is full of precious things, one will never be able to preserve them.

When one is wealthy, high ranking, and proud of himself, he invites misfortune.

In other words, the way of the Tao is *reversal*. The greater the effort to impose a rigid structure that protects and enriches the few, the greater the reversal will be. In the Taoist perspective, this law of the universe manifests in both our inner world of experience and the external world of wealth and political power.

To summarize: systems provide an external structure—an account about how the world works--and an internal experience of living in the system. While the system may be described in abstract language, our experience of living in the system is very real. But to fully understand a system, we can't just look at its abstract account of how the world works; we have to explore the experience of living within the system, i.e. what the system enables or discourages in individuals' lives.

Leverage Points in Systems

Three decades after my university studies, my stock-trading mentor Harun Ibrahim sent me Donella Meadows' seminal essay on systems, *Leverage Points: Places to intervene in a System* (1999).

The three philosophic systems I very briefly sketched out above (my interpretations, by the way) are based on cause and effect—even mystical Taoism rests on cause and effect—but what Meadows illuminates is *the opportunities to change the system's results with small modifications.*

In other words, when we want to change what the system produces, we don't necessarily have to change everything. In most cases, modifying just one element changes the system's results because this one element is a *point of leverage.*

As Meadows explains, one way to change a system is to add a *feedback loop*, a new pathway for information and transactions that wasn't there before.

As an example, consider a corrupt tax collection system in which citizens must wait in long lines to pay their taxes to agents, all of whom collect bribes to insure the payment is properly credited. Citizens who don't pay a bribe might find their tax payment has "gone missing," and now they owe penalties which will require additional bribes to resolve.

In such a system, there is no escape from corruption, which has become so entrenched that tax agents' salaries are kept artificially low because it's expected they'll receive much of their "salary" in the form of bribes. (In an irony typical of corrupt systems, since the bribes are paid under the table, they're not taxable.)

A conventional reformer might propose penalties on accepting bribes, a more rigorous process to screen out corrupt agents, a new bureaucracy to oversee the tax collection agency, and so on. But all these extraordinarily costly and cumbersome reforms won't actually eliminate bribery and corruption; all that's been added is another layer of bribery that must be paid to the new overseers, and so the net result is that the dysfunctional system becomes even more dysfunctional.

In Meadows' analysis, this counter-productive "solution that makes the problem worse" is the default setting of institutions: *"Leverage points are not intuitive. Or if they are, we intuitively use them backward, systematically worsening whatever problems we are trying to solve."*

The way to eliminate the inequities of tax collection corruption is to *add a feedback loop that bypasses the tax agents entirely*: a simple mobile phone application that works on even the lowest cost phones to make tax payments directly from an online account to the tax agency. Not only does this new feedback loop eliminate the necessity of paying bribes, it also lowers the entire system's cost by eliminating the majority of the human agents and the bureaucracy overseeing the agents.

There is an almost Taoist quality to the irony that conventional solutions only make the problem worse because they add complexity and cost without adding any new feedback loops.

As for the global economy and the conventional solutions to endemic poverty, Meadows writes: "The world's leaders are correctly fixated on economic growth as the answer to virtually all problems, but they're pushing with all their might in the wrong direction."

Writer Clay Shirky made much the same point: *"Institutions will try to preserve the problem to which they are the solution."* In other words, those benefiting from the continued failure of conventional solutions have every incentive to continue adding more cost and complexity because this gives them job security.

In addition to self-interest, there's also an institutional bias in favor of finding problems that can be solved with existing systems and ignoring those that can't. As *Wired* magazine co-founder Kevin Kelly observed, *"Established industries like to focus on established problems."* In other words, there are extremely strong forces within institutions that will resist adding leverage points (new feedback loops, etc.) for fear that they would lose control of the system that benefits them so mightily. In a Taoist dynamic, this rigid protection of systemic privilege leads to the collapse of the entire system, since systems that sacrifice flexibility and adaptability to maintain the status quo are brittle—a topic we'll discuss shortly.

Hierarchical and Self-Organizing Systems

What can we learn from these ideas that could help us design a system that wouldn't fall into the usual institutional quicksand described by Meadows, Shirky and Kelly?

First, economy and society are two sides of one coin: a just, fair society cannot arise from an exploitive, unfair economy. The economy must itself be all the things we want in our society.

Second, the rules of conduct for members of our new system must be easy-to-understand guidelines all agree to follow: in essence, treat everyone as you want to be treated, and don't hog the ball; play for the team.

Third, those who govern least govern best. Since our alternative system will be democratic, this means governing by trust rather than fear, and by cooperation rather than coercion.

Those who believe human nature is essentially evil and that people become cruel and abusive without rigid controls reckon that William Golding's novel *Lord of the Flies* got it right: once freed of strict authority, humans quickly degrade into savagery. In Golding's story, a group of teenage boys are cast away on an island. Without the strict order imposed by adults, the stronger and more aggressive boys soon dominate and torture the weaker, younger boys, and things go downhill from there.

But reality is quite the opposite, which we know from an unplanned real-world experiment that mimicked Goldman's teen castaways almost perfectly. The *Guardian (UK)* newspaper article *The real Lord of the Flies: what happened when six boys were shipwrecked for 15 months* by Rutger Bregman restored a forgotten bit of history. In 1966, six teenage boys whose crippled fishing boat drifted onto an uninhabited island in the South Pacific that had once been inhabited didn't just survive; they thrived. At first the boys struggled until they climbed to the top of the 1,000 foot mountain and discovered wild chickens, banana and taro plants left from the previous inhabitants a century before.

The teens organized themselves into teams of two, sharing responsibility for the garden, kitchen and guard duty. Occasional disagreements were settled by a mutually agreed cooling off period. The ship captain who happened upon the remote island 15 months later reported that "the boys had set up a small commune with food garden, hollowed-out tree trunks to store rainwater, a gymnasium with curious weights, a badminton court, chicken pens and a permanent fire, all from handiwork, an old knife blade and much determination."

There is a shelf full of science to support what happened on the island: *cooperation*, not because they were coerced by authorities, but because it was their natural response and so obviously beneficial to everyone. Friendly competition has a role, of course (hence the rough-and-ready badminton court) but from birth humans are instinctively attuned to social cues and the expectations of others.

This unplanned real-world experiment also illustrates another key feature of systems: systems can be *hierarchical*, like an army's top-down structure with generals at the top giving orders to officers who then give orders to soldiers, or they can be *self-organizing*, where participants generate a dynamic equilibrium without a top authority figure issuing orders.

Hierarchies are centralized command systems, where reports go up the chain of command and orders flow down. You can't have a decentralized (i.e. every group is equal so there is no top dog ordering everyone else around) hierarchy, nor can you have a voluntary hierarchy in which everyone is free to decide whether to obey the commands from the top or not. (Joining the hierarchy may be voluntary, but once you're in the system, your compliance is mandatory.)

In self-organizing systems, there is no top-down chain of command. There is no general passing orders to officers who then tell the privates what to do. Each part of the network adjusts and adapts based on feedback from other parts.

The difference between centralized hierarchies and self-organizing systems is clear when systems expand. Self-organizing systems add new units without having to add a new layer of management; each unit manages itself and its integration into the system. Nature is a self-organizing system; the animals and plants introduced by humans a century before the boys were shipwrecked became part of the island's ecosystem without any human hierarchy controlling the process.

Self-organizing systems expand by following the same rules that they used to organize in the first place. There's a term for this ability to scale up (become larger) by repeating the same rules and patterns: *scale-invariance*.

The same elements that make up the ecosystem around a single fern—the soil composition, bacteria, worms, insects, birds, lizards, etc.—will organize life in 100 square meters of ferns, 1,000 square meters, or 10 square kilometers. The size (scale) of the system doesn't change how the system organizes itself.

Hierarchies, on the other hand, require additional management as the system expands. When the army adds new units of soldiers, the number of junior and senior officers must also expand, along with civilian managers to handle the increasing flow of food, fuel, ammunition, etc. The number of orders expands as well, requiring multitudes of additional workers to process all the communications. Most hierarchies (what we call *bureaucracies*) add more managers in every layer because the system requires more orders flowing down from the top and more staff to make sure lower levels comply.

If we look at human history, it's clear that the large-scale miseries humans impose on each other are the result of coercive, centrally-controlled hierarchies. Without a top-down coercive system, no small group at the top could exploit human society so ruthlessly.

Ideologies require coercive hierarchies to enforce compliance with the doctrines of the day. Thousands of loyal cadres were imprisoned or executed by the Soviet and Chinese Communist Parties because they happened to be loyal to party functionaries who were suspected of disloyalty to the top leaders.

Exploitive systems such as colonialism are also coercive hierarchies, with the handful of plantation owners reaping the gains from poorly paid employees by imposing their rule with armed force.

It's worth noting that ideologically organized hierarchies typically claim to be pursuing highly idealistic visions of a perfect society of perfect humans—if only everyone follows the orders from the top. Failure to believe with sufficient sincerity, failure to follow orders with sufficient enthusiasm, or failure to renounce one's doubts are all grounds for censure, imprisonment or worse. The idealized goal of ideologies—to impose perfection on an imperfect world—then justifies every cruelty since the goal is so worthy: *the idealized ends justify any means* of reaching the perfect world, including torture, imprisonment and execution.

Alternatively, if humans self-organize into small groups such as farming hamlets, local businesses and community organizations, etc., no one group has enough power to subjugate other groups with a rigid ideology or exploitive hierarchy. Voluntary, self-organizing groups cannot impose a cruel doctrine because members will simply quit. Nor can they aspire to imposing some idealistic dictatorship on everyone else. The ideal in self-organizing systems is *incremental improvement and adaptation*: rather than throw every imperfect human into a grinder in a vain reach for a perfect world, self-organizing systems are constantly experimenting with small, incremental advances. This process is one of generating a steady churn of experiments and feedback to discover which variations work and which ones don't.

Self-organizing systems are not rigid; the experimentation and feedback generate a constant ferment which fuels adapting to new conditions and adopting incremental improvements.

Small, self-organizing groups naturally express a variety of opinions and goals because there is no coercive hierarchy to suppress a variety of views. This variety and lack of centralized control makes voluntary self-organized groups much more resilient, flexible and adaptive—in other words, much more likely to overcome challenges that shatter rigid, centralized hierarchies.

The Weakness of Centralized Hierarchical Systems

Centralized hierarchies are essential to imposing monarchies, dictatorships, totalitarianism, religious theocracies and exploitive colonialism on unwilling subjects. Any system ruled by one person or a small elite must have a pyramid-shaped hierarchy to force compliance on everyone in the system, right down to the lowest level.

The inherent weakness of this highly centralized command structure was memorably summarized by a line in Pete Townsend's 1971 song *Won't Get Fooled Again*: *meet the new boss, same as the old boss*. Anyone who manages to overthrow those at the top of the pyramid can take over the entire system, becoming the new boss.

The immense concentration of wealth and power at the top of a centralized hierarchy is an irresistible temptation to those seeking instant wealth and power, and the greater the concentration of power, the greater the temptation. Hence the endless parade of Roman emperors who ascended to the throne by assassinating the previous emperor. Predictably, most met the same fate at the hands of the next usurper.

Edward Luttwak's 1968 book, *Coup d'Etat, A Practical Handbook*, lays out how a small elite can replace the nation's existing elite and take over the entire centralized hierarchy. *Meet the new boss, same as the old boss*.

Compare this ever-so-tempting path to instant wealth and power to the impossibility of a small group taking complete control of a self-organizing system. Since there is no pyramid with a tiny elite at the top commanding everyone below, there is no way to seize power. Self-organizing systems are immune to autocracies and exploitive hierarchies. There can't be any *new boss* because there isn't any *old boss*.

Anti-Fragile Systems

Author Nassim Taleb contributed a key insight into the nature of systems with his work on *anti-fragile* structures, which as noted in a previous section, get stronger when they encounter shocks that cause fragile systems to collapse.

Taleb distinguishes between systems that survive volatile crises (what he calls *resilient systems*) and those which don't just survive but thrive, what he calls *anti-fragile systems*—rather than being weakened by crises, they're strengthened, becoming better prepared to handle whatever is thrown at them as a result of confronting the crisis.

The castaway boys on the island became stronger physically and emerged with greater emotional and social capital. Rather than just survive, they thrived. Through cooperation, ingenuity and hard work, they fashioned successful workarounds to all the life-threatening challenges, despite having few tools or other resources.

One way to see the difference between fragile systems like centralized hierarchies and anti-fragile systems is to examine the links between the various parts. Centralized hierarchies are *tightly bound* (a concept mentioned previously) while anti-fragile systems are *loosely bound*.

The links in tightly bound systems all pass through a small number of *nodes* in the network. Examples of nodes include mobile phone signal transmitters, docks where container ships unload their containers, railway stations, and servers in a company's digital network.

Global supply chains offer examples of the two types of systems.

Imagine a factory in Asia that assembles laptop computers. To get the lowest possible cost, the factory sources each component from one supplier—the one offering the lowest price. It then transports the assembled laptops for delivery via one shipper, who uses one harbor and one shipping line to deliver the laptops to North America. The products are then offloaded by one firm which distributes all the laptops from a single warehouse.

This system is *tightly bound* because the failure of any one node will bring down the whole system. If one component supplier goes broke and shuts down, or there's a fire in the factory, or a strike at the harbor or a disruption at the distribution warehouse, the supply chain is broken and the laptops are no longer available to customers.

A *loosely bound* supply system maintains multiple suppliers for each component, multiple shippers for shipments and multiple distributors at the end of the chain, even if all this duplication and redundancy costs a bit more. If any node in this system fails, the disruption is not catastrophic; the other suppliers and shippers can pick up the slack. Any disruption is temporary.

You'll recall our previous discussions of workarounds and self-organizing systems. Workarounds are cumbersome in tightly bound systems, and easy in loosely bound systems, which are basically designed with workarounds in mind.

Self-organizing systems are by their very mature loosely bound, as each part has links and feedbacks with every other part. If a node shared by different groups fails, they already have links to alternative nodes.

The Internet is a global example of a self-organizing system in which participants agree on basic rules of use and conduct. Anyone can add a node to the network as long as it uses the shared protocols and follows the rules. If any node fails, Internet traffic is routed through other nodes.

Since the Internet is self-organizing and loosely bound, it is resilient, adaptive and anti-fragile.

We can now add three more points about our alternative system: it must be self-organizing and cooperative by nature, voluntary rather than coercive, and it must be anti-fragile, becoming more adaptable as it encounters volatility.

To Change a System, You Must Change the Values and Processes

The most important thing I've learned about systems is this: *if we don't change a system's values and processes, then we haven't changed anything.* Every system manifests a set of values which is expressed by what the system's processes optimize and what it doesn't measure.

Those benefiting from the system will naturally say it expresses the most wonderful values, even as the system rewards the few at the expense of the many. To understand what the system actually values, we have to look at what its processes actually produce. If the system's processes produce unfairness, that reflects the system's built-in values.

Using the corrupt tax collection system as an example, those benefiting from the system will defend it as the *only possible way to collect taxes*. They will also promote reforms that don't actually change processes or values. We saw that adding another layer of oversight didn't change the process of corruption (with taxpayers standing in line and having to bribe underpaid civil servants); it simply extended the opportunities for additional bribery. Nor did it change the exploitation of taxpayers who had no alternative to the corrupt system.

Even adding a new feedback loop doesn't necessarily change the system's values and processes. To actually change the system's results, a new feedback loop has to change the system's core processes so they manifest a new set of values. The only way to change the tax collection system's values is to bypass bribery and corrupt oversight. This structural change is the only way to change what the system produces from *unfair* to *fair*.

To change a system, we first have to be forthright about what it actually values by looking at what its processes produce. Then we have to choose another set of values that we want the processes to manifest, and design processes that will produce the values we seek.

This is *the hacker's teleology*: connect the dots of values, processes and systems by designing a work-around so the processes produce the values we seek.

What Kind of System Do We Want to Live In?

No elite will ever admit the system they rule has failed the non-elites. They will tout its remarkable success and permanence even as it is swept into oblivion because to be honest about the failings might trigger a loss of faith in their rule. Ironically, this unwillingness to face problems squarely hastens the system's collapse, because denial and half-measures cannot solve systemic problems.

Whether the system is failing or not depends on *what we measure* and *what we value*. An autocratic system that rewards the few at the top at the expense of the many is very successful to those being enriched and an utter failure to those being exploited. The U.S. economy, for example, is constantly touted as a success because it continues to expand when measured by gross domestic product (GDP). But if we measure what the wages of the bottom 95% can buy, the economy is a failure, as their wages buy far less healthcare, housing, education and childcare than they did 20 years ago.

In other words, all the gains of the economy have flowed to the top while the bottom 95% have lost ground. This becomes obvious once we measure the cost of healthcare, housing, childcare, college, etc. by the *number of hours of labor required to pay for it*. Since it takes far more hours of labor to pay these expenses, we're falling behind, regardless of what the GDP may be.

If we look at who has gained income and wealth, the majority of the gains have flowed to the top 0.1% of American households. A lesser amount went to the rest of the top 1% and a modest amount went to the rest of the top 5%.

The top 5% have a big incentive to hide this reality behind a flurry of positive-looking statistics such as GDP.

Measuring Success or Failure: The Chinese Example

What each socio-economic group values also affects the calculation of success or failure. China is a good example to illustrate this.

As a young teen I'd read everything I could find on China in the late 1960s, which was very sparse because the country was closed to the outside world in the catastrophic Cultural Revolution, which lasted from 1966 to 1976 when Mao died. I was fascinated by the revolutionary zeal and idealism that inspired enormous systemic changes in China such as rural communes and *barefoot doctors*, lightly trained cadres who brought minimal medical care to remote villages where there was previously no medical services at all.

This idealism was squandered on disastrous policies (The Great Leap Forward, etc.) that cost millions their lives and set the country back, and the frustrations of these failures helped fuel the destructive extremes of the Cultural Revolution, which destroyed a generation and reversed whatever modest gains had been made since the Communist Party rose to power.

The first Americans to visit China in 1977 after Mao Zedong died were struck by the uniformity of the populace—everyone wore the same Mao jackets and had the same haircuts—and the same low standard of living. By American standards, China's economy was a gargantuan failure.

But if China's leadership valued conformity, an absence of dissent and economic self-sufficiency above all else, then China's system in 1977 was a great success. (The Communist Party's elite enjoyed luxuries unavailable to the bottom 99.99%, of course, another factor in assessing success: *the system is working great for us, so it must be working great for everyone else, too.*)

In the early 1980s, China's leadership rejected the conformity and poverty of the post-Cultural Revolution era in favor of a state-run, globalized economy that was open to free-market entrepreneurism.

When I first visited China in 2000, just 23 years after its first tentative steps of opening up to the outside world, urban China had transformed into a consumerist paradise of gleaming skyscrapers and jam-packed shopping districts filled with young people pursuing their ambitions. If we value the individual's opportunity to get ahead, then clearly the Chinese system in 2000 was more successful than the 1977 version, where opportunities to move to another city, get into college, start a business, etc. were severely limited.

We were fortunate enough to make friends with many immigrants from China, and we heard their firsthand accounts of how their families suffered during the Cultural Revolution. Loyal Army officers were imprisoned as if they were common criminals, the cream of China's acrobats were placed under house arrest for years, and so on. Untold thousands were tortured or killed, or died in captivity. It is still informally forbidden to mention the Cultural Revolution in China, as it reflects so poorly on the Communist system.

I've noted that systems have an *internal structure* of ideas and values and an *external structure* of authority and economic processes. We can assess the success or failure of a system in a similar way: we can assess the results of the *external structure* with an easy-to-measure statistical accounting—household income, GDP, etc. —and assess the success or failure of the *internal structure* by asking questions about how easy or difficult is it for a typical resident to get ahead—or at least feel like they're getting ahead.

Basic questions about *opportunities to get ahead* include: what does the system encourage, allow, or make difficult? How easy it to move to another locale, get more education, recruit a mentor, start an enterprise, build social capital, find a job, hire employees, protect your ideas, satisfy all government regulations? How easy or difficult is it to *reinvent yourself*? How many opportunities are there for those without any privilege to fashion *workarounds* when the conventional paths are crowded or blocked?

On a deeper level, how easy or difficult is it to be your authentic self and fulfill your ambitions? Does the system discourage or encourage *agency* (i.e. taking charge of your life) and connecting the dots of your experiences in unconventional ways?

For such an assessment to be accurate, these types of questions should be answered by average people, not just those in privileged positions.

We must also ask: what kind of fairness does the system reflect in the everyday life of non-elites? Does daily life consist of a double standard, i.e. one set of rules for the bottom 95% and another set for the top 5%? Is daily life dominated by various types of corruption and extortion that favor the few at the expense of the many?

What costs fall on those who maintain high ethical standards? Are they ridiculed, marginalized, or imprisoned, or are they rewarded and respected?

We also have to ask questions that go beyond the usual official statistics of growth: how many resources are consumed to get the growth? What costs such as pollution aren't being measured?

Does the system benefit everyone more or less equally, or do the majority of the benefits go to those at the top? Does everyone have equal access or clean air, water, healthy food and basic healthcare, or are these only available to the privileged few at the top?

Once we have answers in hand, the final question is: is this a system you want to live in? Is it fair, just and full of opportunities for the many, or is it rigged to benefit the few at the expense of the many?

If the existing system isn't one we want to live in, maybe it's time for us to create an alternative system that we do want to live in.

Section Five:
How Money Is Created and Distributed

As noted earlier, society reflects the economy. If the financial system is unfair, then society will also be unfair. If we want a fair, opportunities-for-all society, we need to look at how money is created and distributed, because this is the foundation of the economy.

If the system for creating money is rigged to benefit the few, then the entire economy will also be rigged to benefit the few, and society will be unfair and corrupt—exactly what we have now.

In this section we'll look at a very difficult topic: how money is created and distributed, and how it's rigged to enrich those at the top and exploit everyone else.

What's interesting about money is that almost everyone is interested in getting more of it but almost no one is interested in how money is created and distributed—in other the words, *the system of money*.

Defenders of the current money system naturally claim this is *the only possible way to create and distribute money*, but this is false. Our system's process for creating and distributing money is deeply unfair. It rigs the entire system to benefit the few at the top at the expense of everyone else.

From the point of view of the individual, money might look like a self-organizing system: money is borrowed and changes hands in millions of transactions between individuals, households, businesses and government agencies, and nobody appears to be coerced to do anything other than earn a livelihood or find a way to get money from the government.

All these transactions are how money flows through the economy, but this isn't how *money is created and distributed*. Money is created and distributed only to those at the very tip-top of the financial pyramid. Those at the top get all the newly issued money which they then use to effortlessly make more money. Those of us at the bottom only get a dribble of the newly issued money if we pay *interest* for the privilege of *borrowing some of the money* insiders got for free.

Can this terribly unfair system actually be the way money is created and distributed? Yes, it is. This is a difficult system to understand, but bear with me. The effort will be well worth it.

How Banks Create Money

There's an old joke about bankers. As the loan applicant is about to enter the bank manager's office, a friendly employee offered a helpful suggestion: the manager has a glass eye, and it's imperative that you look at his good eye. The applicant asks, "How can I tell the glass eye from the good eye?" The employee replies, "The glass eye has a twinkle of warmth."

As I drove through Waimea's morning mist to my appointment with the branch manager of the First Hawaiian Bank, I wasn't thinking of banker jokes; my thoughts were of windows: the driver-side window in my old VW Beetle, which had slipped down into the door panel due to the crank mechanism rusting out, and the window openings in my half-built house that were covered with stapled sheets of plastic that flapped loudly in the wind at night.

Since I'd sunk every dollar into my first building project, there was no money to get the VW's window fixed or to buy windows for the half-finished house. I needed a chunk of cash to get it done and I didn't have it. Yes, I was doing small construction jobs to earn money, but at this rate I'd be gray-haired by the time I had enough cash to complete the house, which at that time had only a roof, a kitchen sink, a barebones bathroom and little else. The floor was bare plywood, the interior walls were unpainted drywall, and our furniture consisted of a cheap folding futon bed and a peeling wood-frame sofa donated by a neighbor.

A conventional mortgage was out of the question because borrowers needed a regular full-time job to qualify. My only hope was to convince my local banker that I could finish the house with a personal loan and somehow pay it back despite being only marginally employed. It was a tall order, since I was all of 26, as green as the grass covering the wind-swept hills, had no credentials other a degree in philosophy (try getting a loan based on that!) and a half-finished house that nobody in their right mind would put much value on. People generally want finished houses, not half-finished ones.

This was my first contact with banking, and my focus was on getting the loan, not on *where the money comes from*. That would come later, when the housing bubble in the early 2000s expanded to previously unimaginable heights. That's when I learned the funny thing about *money*: everybody's interested in getting more of it, but when you start talking about how *money is created*, their eyes glaze over, as if *where money comes from* is the most boring topic on Earth. But it shouldn't be, since it has everything to do with who gets the money (banks, financiers and corporations) and who doesn't (the rest of us), and who gets rich as a result of this system (not us).

Let's imagine a special black box with near-magical powers: it prints real money, not counterfeit bills, but real honest-to-goodness U.S. dollars. You hook it up to a computer, it creates dollars out of thin air and deposits them in your bank account.

Wait, you say; there must be a catch. You're right, there is: you can't spend any of the newly created cash, but if you buy a government bond that pays interest, you get to spend the interest.

So you create $1 million out of thin air and buy bonds that pay 3% interest. Now you're getting $30,000 a year for doing absolutely nothing. Definitely a sweet deal, but why not create more money and earn even more? So you create another $99 million, and now you're earning $3 million a year for doing nothing other than having the magic black box.

That's how money is created in our financial system.

No way, you exclaim; you're joking, right? No, that's exactly how the Federal Reserve, a.k.a. The Fed, our privately owned, quasi-public central bank, creates money out of thin air. All central banks create their currencies in the same way, and they use the new money to buy bonds and other assets.

The current Federal Reserve Chair Jerome Powell said this very clearly in a May 17, 2020 interview on the TV program *60 Minutes*. When the interviewer asked, "*Where does the money come from? Do you just print it?*" Powell answered: "*We print it digitally. So as a central bank, we have the ability to create money digitally. And we do that by buying Treasury Bills or bonds... and that actually increases the money supply.*"

The Federal Reserve's black box digitally printed $3.5 trillion after the global financial crisis of 2008-09, and bought $2 trillion in U.S. Treasury bonds and $1.5 trillion in mortgage-backed securities, i.e. batches of home mortgages. They created about $10,600 out of thin air for each and every one of us 330 million Americans.

You didn't get a check for $10,600 from the Federal Reserve. This newly issued money didn't go to individual Americans. It bailed out the banks and wealthy financiers whose frauds had torpedoed the U.S. economy. (Federal Reserve spokespeople denied this, of course, but it would hardly do to admit to the unfairness of our money system, the corruption of our financial elite or the Fed's role in bailing them out.)

But that's just central banks, you say; private banks can't create money out of thin air. Actually, they do. Here's how it works.

Let's say you own a bank—congratulations. You now own a money-printing black box called *fractional reserve banking*. What does this mean? It means if your bank has $10,000 in cash deposits, you can create $300,000 out of thin air by issuing a loan, for example, a mortgage.

Hold on, you say; don't banks lend the cash deposited by customers? No, they create the money they lend out of thin air. The *fractional reserve banking* black box only requires the bank to hold a *fraction* of each loan in cash—what's known as a *reserve.*

Let's say I deposit $10,000 in your bank. This becomes your bank's cash *reserves.*

This cash is set aside to cover customer withdrawals or losses from borrowers who stop making their loan payments (i.e. borrowers who *default*).

Bank regulations require you to keep 3% of your loans in cash reserves. This means your bank can issue a $300,000 mortgage to a customer, because 3% of $300,000 is $9,000, and you've got $10,000 in reserves.

You're not loaning the cash deposited by savers; you're creating the money out of thin air.

This is a sweet deal because you're charging interest on all these loans. You get to keep all the interest earned by the money you created out of nothing.

Note that banks *borrow money into existence*. But the money created by issuing a loan is a debt that must be paid back with interest.

So those with the power to *borrow money into existence* get the interest due on the loans. They don't have to invent something or start a new enterprise to make money; they just need a qualified borrower who wants a loan. If they can't find a qualified borrower who wants a loan, they can't create money out of thin air and collect interest. Their magic black box can't create new money without borrowers.

Lending money to borrowers who may default (i.e. stop making loan payments) is not a good idea because (1) the bank no longer collects the interest income; and (2) the bank is on the hook for the loan: it has to absorb this loss. If the bank loans someone $10,000 and they stop paying, the bank has to write off the $10,000 as a loss.

Banks want to earn interest (money), not lose money, so they screen borrowers to find creditworthy folks with stable incomes and a history of making payments on previous loans. The banks also want *collateral*, some real-world asset the borrower pledges to the bank so if the borrower defaults, the bank can seize the asset and sell it.

For a mortgage, the collateral pledged is the house the borrower is buying. For an auto loan, it's the car.

There are two important points here:

1) If nobody wants to borrow money, the banks can't create money and earn interest on it; the whole machine grinds to a halt. The banks have to find qualified borrowers who want loans or they can't make money. If creditworthy people *don't want to borrow money*, the machine grinds to a halt.

2) There is always a risk that the borrower will default and the bank will lose money, and so the bank is happiest loaning money to rich people and profitable companies because they have plenty of income and plenty of assets to pledge as collateral. The bank is not happy if the only people who want to borrow money have little income or collateral, because these people are more likely to default, which forces the bank to take a big loss.

This is why there's a saying, *if you want a bank loan, prove you don't need the money*. This is why rich people can borrow money if they want to, and people who aren't rich have trouble qualifying for loans.

This was why I was so anxious about going to the bank to beg for a loan: I didn't have the secure income or the collateral (a 100% completed house) that banks look for. I was the kind of customer they avoided like the plague: insecure income and not much collateral.

The Rate of Interest You Pay Determines If You're Rich or Poor

Are you still with me? This hasn't been too painful, right? We're almost done, but we have a few more things to understand about our money system.

First is *the rate of interest*, i.e. how much interest the bank is charging on the loan. The lower the rate of interest, the lower the monthly payment, and the less interest the borrower pays to the bank. Over time, the rate of interest makes a huge difference in who gets rich and remains poor.

As a general rule, the more creditworthy the borrower, the lower the interest rate will be. Borrowers deemed risky have to compensate the bank for the higher risk that the borrower might default on the loan by paying a higher rate of interest.

So the rich get richer because they pay a lower rate of interest and the poor get poorer because they pay a higher rate of interest for the same loan.

Let's say you get a 1% interest auto loan for $20,000, and I get a 10% interest loan for the same loan. (Note that all the interest rates I'm using here are for illustration purposes only; they're not intended to reflect actual auto loan or mortgage rates.) Over the seven-year term of the loan, you'll pay about $700 in interest and I'll pay around $7,800. That's a **big** difference. I'm going to pay $7,000 more to the bank, leaving less of my income to save or spend on other things.

Now let's say we each get a standard 30-year home mortgage of $200,000. My interest rate is 5.5%, so I'll actually end up paying more in interest ($208,000) than the mortgage ($200,000). But you got a $200,000 mortgage at only a 1.5% interest rate, so the total interest you'll pay after 30 years is $48,000, which means over the 30 years, compared to me, you'll save $160,000 to invest or spend on other things.

(Those who think a 1.5% interest mortgage is impossible might recall that billionaire Mark Zuckerberg got a 1% interest mortgage a few years ago. Why would a billionaire want a mortgage when he's swimming in cash? Because getting a low-interest loan leaves his cash available to earn higher interest elsewhere. The rich get rich (and richer) by being savvy about money.)

On the face of it, the bank makes a lot more money by making a loan to someone paying 5.5% than 1.5%—but the bank has to factor in the risk of default: loaning $200,000 to someone who might default would be a bad bet because the bank might lose tens of thousands of dollars.

This takes us back to *if you want a bank loan, prove you don't need the money*: the bank is willing to get less interest from a wealthy borrower because the risk of losing money is so low. If the borrower is not very creditworthy, then the bank says, hmm, if we charge a lot more interest, this bet is worth taking.

Now flash back to our false assumption that *banks loan out cash deposited by savers*. If this were the case, the bank would have to choose which loan to make because there was only so much cash to lend out. But since banks can issue as many loans as they want as long as they set aside 3% of their deposits in reserves, banks can issue loans to rich and poor alike. The only difference is in the interest rate being charged: low risk = low interest (rich people); high risk = high interest (poorer people).

So rich people pay less interest and get to keep more of their income for other purposes, and poor people pay more interest and end up with much less of their income for other purposes. *The rich get richer, the poor get poorer*: this is the inevitable result of our current money system.

The Rich Outbid Everyone Else

To get a fuller picture of this, let's say my household has lived frugally and saved up the $50,000 down payment for an income-producing property, a rental house that costs $250,000. The $50,000 earns very little in a savings account, but if it's invested in a rental, it could earn a lot more. Buying a rental home would give our frugal family *unearned income, money made by money* rather than from working for wages (*earned income*).

In this scenario, using the $50,000 down payment, let's say my household qualifies for a mortgage of $200,000 at 4.5% interest. The monthly cost of owning the rental is around $1,600 for the mortgage payment (interest and principal), property taxes, insurance, maintenance and utilities. If the house can be rented for $2,000 a month, our frugal household could earn $400 a month—far more than the few dollars earned by the $50,000 in a savings account.

But a rich family is also bidding on the property, and since they have a big income and plenty of collateral, they qualify for a 1.5% mortgage. Their total monthly expenses are around $1,300, a lot less than the frugal family due to the lower interest rate. Since their costs are lower, the rich family can outbid my frugal family, offering $300,000 for the rental home. Offering a higher bid raises their monthly expenses to $1,475, still less than my frugal household's cost.

Do you see the life-changing difference in getting lower rates of interest? The rich family can outbid the frugal family and still make more monthly profit from the rental home than the frugal family could if they'd bought the house for $250,000.

Since $300,000 is more than the frugal family can afford, they lose the chance to buy the rental property. Even if they stretched their finances to the limit and bid $300,000, their monthly net profit would be paper-thin because they're paying more in interest than the rich family.

Do you see the enormous advantage of low-interest loans? Not only can the rich family outbid the frugal family for assets that generate unearned income—*money making money*—they make more every month even after outbidding the frugal family.

The rich get richer, the poor get poorer is a direct result of the system we have for *creating and distributing money*: the rich can borrow more money at much lower rates of interest than poor people can, so the rich can buy assets that produce investment (unearned) income—*money making money.*

Since the poor pay higher rates of interest, they pay more of their income to banks than rich people do, and keep less of their income for other purposes such as saving up a nest egg. The higher interest payments are a headwind to saving enough money to buy the assets that the rich buy to get richer.

It's been a slog, but now we understand why *the rich get richer, the poor get poorer*. There really isn't any other possible outcome given the way the current money system works.

Where the New Money Goes: Into the Pockets of the Rich

There's one more wrinkle we have to understand before we leave the eye-glazing topic of our *money system*. Let's return to the central bank's money printing black box for a moment and follow *where the money goes*.

Let's say our economy has a total money supply of $1 million, meaning there is $1 million in paper bills, coins and cash in bank accounts. This money circulates as people buy and sell, pay their employees and so on.

The central bank plugs in its magic black box and creates another $1 million out of thin air. This doubles the money supply of our small economy from $1 million to $2 million. Where does this new money go?

The central bank buys $1 million of bonds from rich people. (In the real economy, the Fed buys bonds from a special class of financiers called *broker-dealers*, but it boils down to essentially the same thing.) The central bank now owns $1 million in bonds, and the rich people have $1 million in cash which they can use to buy other assets.

Was the $1 million in new money distributed to everyone equally? No; it only went to rich people, who can use it to buy assets that earn income: rental property, stocks that pay dividends and so on.

Did increasing the amount of money in the economy help the poor people? No. The only way they can get any of this new money is to borrow it and pay interest, enriching the banks in the process.

But wait, you say: is it really this simple?

Yes. This is the way money is created and distributed in our financial system, and the only outcome is the rich get richer and the poor get poorer. The money that's created out of thin air goes only to the top of the pyramid, to banks, corporations and super-wealthy financiers. None of it goes to the bottom 99.9%. The only access the 99.9% have to newly created money is to borrow it, at much higher rates of interest than rich people pay.

I know, I know—you want to believe the system isn't rigged to favor banks and the rich, but it is. You want to believe the playing field is level, but it isn't. You want to believe everyone has the same chance to get ahead, but they don't.

The system gives banks the power to create money out of thin air, and this freshly issued money goes to the wealthy, who then buy up the assets that generate unearned income: *money made with money*.

All banks need to get rich is a black box that creates money out of thin air, and all rich people need is access to low-interest loans. They don't have to create any value in the real economy or risk starting a new business.

For poor people to get rich, they have to *create value in the real economy* by working hard and accepting the risk of losing everything they worked for. Banks don't lend money to risky new ventures like Apple, which was famously started in a garage by the two Steves, Jobs and Wozniak. Why take a risk on young guys with no track record? The pair raised Apple's first $1,000 of working capital by selling their most valuable possessions, an old van and a costly calculator.

All of which brings us back, finally, to me, the green 26-year old trying to get a bank loan to finish his first building project. The bank manager wanted to give me a loan, as that's how banks make money. But he had to convince the loan department that my project was a reasonable risk to take. Recall that *if you want a bank loan, prove you don't need the money,* and I couldn't do that.

Risk, Greed and Socially Useless Activity

Let's step back for a moment and look at two assumptions that are routinely made about our financial system. One is that *everyone seeking to maximize their profit benefits everyone*: if every individual and company chooses whatever makes them the most profit, the whole system will magically benefit everyone. Apple is cited as an example of how this works: Apple maximized profits by inventing the iPhone, which benefits society at large.

In other words, greed ends up generating *socially useful goods and services*. Greed isn't just good for the greedy, it's good for everyone else, too.

The second assumption is that *risk is rewarded*. Those plucky Steves raised $1,000 by selling their most valuable possessions, took big risks and were rewarded with fabulous riches.

These assumptions are the bedrock of our society and economy. If greedy rich people only benefit themselves at the expense of society, and they get richer by avoiding risk, then what happened to the *level playing field/equal opportunity for all* that's the core premise of our society? If that premise is empty, then *greed is good for everyone* is nothing but a useful illusion to keep the lower 95% from rebelling against a rigged financial system.

At the risk of boring you further, I have to describe the way the really big money is made in our system. It's not by investing in plucky young folks in garages, because the odds of even one striking it rich are low. It's much more likely that gambling millions of dollars on plucky youngsters ends up batting zero, where the money's gone and there's no new Apple.

A much better way to maximize greed is to avoid risk and skim steady profits from the stock market using *High Frequency Trading* (HFT). Even my eyes glaze over describing how this works, so if you really want to understand HFT, please look it up. The basic idea is that by making millions of trades a day, HFT computers can spoof the market into coughing up a tiny gain on each trade. Tiny gains multiplied by millions of trades adds up to low-risk profits for the owners of the HFT computers.

So a low-risk profitable endeavor for a bank is to loan a financier cash to buy faster HFT computers. Greedy bank wins, greedy financier wins, and how about society? Society loses, because this is *socially useless activity*. Alas, *greed isn't good for everyone*, and *risk is not rewarded; avoiding risk is rewarded*.

There's no end to financial tricks like HFT; new ones arise as soon as old ones peter out. Here's a really simple one: borrow money at 2% interest and buy a bond that pays 3%. That 1% for *socially useless activity* works out to $1 million a year for financiers who borrow $100 million. And since the bank makes money on the loan, the bank wins, too, for *socially useless activity*.

Then there are tricks to leverage that $100 million into bets totaling $1 billion, so the $100 million can actually skim $10 million a year - again, for doing absolutely nothing: producing no goods and services, starting no new companies, *nothing*. Society receives zero benefit as the already-super-rich further enrich themselves with tricks that are only available to the super-wealthy.

As noted in the introduction, this is a system that optimizes *anything goes if you're rich enough and winners take all*.

This hurts, doesn't it? We want to believe that our system is all about gutsy youngsters in garages inventing wonderful things that enhance our lives. It's certainly possible to start a business in a garage and get rich despite the long odds, but gambling on long shots is not what our system is about; it's about the built-in privileges of creating money out of thin air and using that money to make more money without having to risk anything.

Our Money System Corrupts the Economy and our Political System

Returning again to the plucky (but alas, no genius) 26-year old trying to scrounge up enough cash to finish his first building project, tattered philosophy degree in hand, let's consider what makes sense to the bank. With a growing population, building a new house or rehabbing an old house is *socially useful activity*. Safe, comfortable housing adds to the wealth of society and brings new supply to the marketplace of buyers and sellers. Anyone building or rehabbing hopes to turn a profit, of course; nobody accepts the risk and sweats the details to lose money.

But what's the safer bet for the bank: a low-risk loan to a wealthy buyer snapping up all the rental homes in town, or taking a chance on a new builder whose project has run out of cash? The logic of the system is undeniable: the big loan to the wealthy buyer of rentals is the prudent and profitable choice. Loaning money to the new (and broke) builder is too risky, and not big enough to make much of a profit for the bank.

What's the social value of rental homes being bought up by one wealthy owner? If the properties were all run down and the new owner invested a lot of money rehabbing them, then that would be socially beneficial. But if the new owner avoids run-down rentals and only buys rentals that need little to no sprucing up, then the social value is negligible.

But there's an even larger social impact of one wealthy owner buying up every available rental in town: that wealthy owner now controls enough of the market to jack up rents without offering any additional value to tenants. This is the power of *monopoly;* the owner can raise the price without offering any increase in quality.

If a small group of owners secretly agree to all raise rents, this is a *cartel*, which has the same market power as a monopoly controlled by one owner.

The social impact of owners jacking up rents is extremely negative. When more of the renter's income is siphoned off to pay higher rents, there is less income left to support local businesses and less money for the renter to save. All the money that could have gone into the local economy goes instead into the pocket of the big owner, who might live thousands of miles away.

If renters can't afford to buy their own homes, they have to rent one of whatever homes are available. They need shelter and can't decide not to rent.

The remaining handful of less greedy landlords will have few vacancies, since their tenants have no incentive to leave their lower-cost rentals. New renters end up with only one choice of landlord: the one who jacked up rents, not because there's a shortage of rentals but because there's *a shortage of rentals owned by less-greedy landlords*.

In theory, some enterprising builder could start building new rental homes and offer lower rents on the new homes. But building new homes takes a long time, and as we've seen, the wealthy owner has the means to outbid everyone else for the new rentals because he has access to low-interest loans.

That's not the end of the social and economic negatives of a wealthy owner buying up a majority of rentals in town. That owner now has more than enough profit to buy political influence by contributing to local politicians' re-election campaigns. One way to maximize his profits would be to limit the construction of additional rentals in town, eliminating potential competition.

So the wealthy owner borrows more money at a low rate of interest and quietly buys up the available building sites. Whatever he can't buy, he uses his influence to persuade the local government to declare as unsuitable for housing via re-zoning.

Note that all of this is perfectly legal: borrowing large sums at low interest rates, outbidding other bidders for rentals, jacking up the rents, buying up all the available house lots, and contributing money to politicians to lock in his monopoly and make him much wealthier than he could have been without political influence.

This hurts, doesn't it? Ours is a *pay-to-play political system* in which cash buys influence, and the way the system creates and distributes money enables the wealthy to build monopolies that extract more of wage-earners' incomes without offering them any additional value.

There's one last point to make here. Profit is easy to measure, but social usefulness is not so easy to measure. (I wrote a whole book called *Will You Be Richer or Poorer?* about how what we measure/don't measure sets our priorities.)

If a system places all the incentives on maximizing profit, regardless of the social and political consequences, then we end up with exactly the system we have now. Our current system is one that rewards socially useless activities, a system rigged to benefit the few who can borrow money that was created out of thin air at low rates of interest.

Remember our fancy word *teleology*? Our system assumes that everyone maximizing their own profit will magically order society to everyone's benefit. We assume greed will automatically create an economy that's beneficial to all.

But this is false: maximizing profit by any means available—greed—doesn't automatically lead to a system that benefits everyone. Given the way our system creates and distributes money, the teleology of maximizing profit leads to the concentration of wealth and power in the hands of the greediest few. And what do people do with this concentrated wealth and power? They use it to accumulate even more wealth and power, increasing inequality to the point that society and the economy start breaking down.

Since *all individuals are equal before the law*, we assume that opportunity is equal, too. But given the way our system creates and distributes money, this is not true: those who can create money or borrow it more cheaply than the rest of us are (to borrow Orwell's phrase) *more equal than others*. It doesn't take creating socially useful products and services to get super-rich; all it takes is being able to create money out of thin air or borrow it at very low rates.

Wishing it wasn't so won't make it so. To change our system, we have to change the way our system creates and distributes money. If we don't change that, we haven't changed anything.

Believing that maximizing profit magically creates *socially useful activity* doesn't make it so. To get *socially useful activity*, we have to start measuring it, because whatever we don't measure is treated like it doesn't exist—even though it clearly does.

The Fantasy: 'We Can Print All the Money We Need'

Central banks can digitally print as much money as they want. This has created the fantasy that if we need more money, the central bank can print as much as we need and distribute the free money to everyone.

This is called Modern Monetary Theory (MMT), and the distribution of free money to everyone is called Universal Basic Income (UBI). Both are very appealing because we all want a free lunch—more money without having to work more.

What if we dispensed with the central bank and just gave everyone the power to print as much money as they wanted at home? Want another $1,000? Just print it at home. But why stop at $1,000? Why not print $10,000, or $100,000 or $1 million? And why not print $1 million every day?

What would happen if everyone could print $1 million at home, every day? I think we all understand that the money would be worthless, because every day the supply of money would go up much faster than the supply of things to buy. While everyone could print more money at home for free, they couldn't create more gasoline, cars or food at home for free.

Why sell a loaf of bread for $1 million when the next buyer might give you $10 million? Why take $10 million when anyone could print $100 million? The seller of bread will quickly decide there's no point in trading a loaf of bread for dollars, and starts asking for payment in tangible things that can't be printed at home: gold, a gallon of gasoline, a bag of flour, etc.

This introduces us to an important feature of money. What we call *price* is the result of the supply of money and the supply of goods and services available to buy. If the supply of money goes up much faster than the supply of things to buy, the amount of money needed to buy a loaf of bread goes up accordingly. When it takes more money to buy a loaf of bread than it did in the past, we call this *inflation*, because the amount of money needed to buy the bread inflated (went up).

Conversely, if the supply of bread goes up faster than the supply of money, it takes less money to buy a loaf of bread. When it takes less money to buy a bread than it did in the past, we call this *deflation*, because the amount of money needed to buy a loaf of bread deflated (went down).

What's scarce rises in value and what's abundant drops in value. If everyone can print money, money is no longer scarce and its value—what it can buy—drops accordingly.

The only way to avoid inflation and deflation is to have the supply of money go up only as much as the supply of goods and services available to buy goes up.

Let's illustrate this with a very simple economic model of loaves of bread—an essential we need to survive—and money.

In an idealized economy, if five loaves of bread are produced, there are five units of money that are each a *claim* on a loaf of bread, meaning that each unit of money can buy a loaf of bread.

To keep things simple, let's say a loaf of bread costs $1, and each unit of money is $1 bill.

Throughout time, a rough balance between the supply of money and the supply of goods/resources was needed to maintain commerce. If there were too few goods, or too little money, then commerce was limited.

In ancient economies, the supply of gold and silver coins—the money of that era—was limited, and so paper money was created in China for small local purchases.

In other words, when there wasn't enough money to grease trade between buyers and sellers, human ingenuity found ways to expand the supply of money to match the expansion of goods available to buy.

So if there are five loaves of bread for sale, but only $1 of money, then the other four can't be sold due to a lack of money. (They can of course be traded for other goods—what we call barter--but money was created to simplify trading different goods by establishing a *means of exchange* everyone could use.)

The solution is to create an additional $4 of money by printing four $1 bills.

What happens when the money supply expands and ten $1 bills are created but there's still only five loaves of bread?

In our example, the first five $1 bills are traded for loaves of bread, and then there's nothing left for the remaining five $1 bills to buy.

Or, alternatively, a bidding war arises for the five loaves of bread. Due to the surplus supply of money in relation to the supply of bread, each dollar is now a claim only on half a loaf of bread. This is devastating to everyone who doesn't have access to the newly created money. Where $1 once bought a loaf of bread, now it only buys half a loaf.

It's much easier to create new claims on bread (money) than it is to produce more loaves of bread. Thus there is an irresistible temptation for those who can create new money to print money to buy up all the bread before the other holders of money catch on to the increase in the supply of money.

But eventually the imbalance between the supply of money and bread is re-balanced by reducing money's claim on loaves of bread. It now takes $2 to buy a loaf of bread. This is inflation. And if enough surplus money is created, then eventually $1 is a claim on only one *slice* of bread.

We call this claim the *purchasing power* of money: never mind the number printed on paper money; how many loaves of bread can you buy with it? If the money purchases less than it did in the past, its *purchasing power* has diminished. This is inflation.

Conventional economists are mystified why inflation has appeared tame over the past 20 years even as the supply of money has increased by trillions of dollars. The answer to their mystery is to follow *who got the trillions of dollars in newly printed money*, and *what did they spend it on*? In other words, it's not just the amount of newly printed money that matters, it's who got the money and what did they spend it on?

In our simplified model of $1 paper bills and loaves of bread, let's say the money supply doubled from ten $1 bills to twenty $1 bills, but every one of the ten new $1 bills ended up in the pocket of one person. After that person buys as much bread as they can eat, their appetite for bread is gone and so they look around for something else that's scarce and that can't be printed up for free like paper money. Ideally, this scarce item can be used to make money, for example, a mill to grind wheat into flour.

So it's critically important to understand who is getting the new money, because whatever they want to buy is what will go up in price.

Very little of the trillions of dollars digitally printed by the Federal Reserve trickled down to wage earners from the financiers, corporations and banks that got the money. The wages of the bottom 95% of households haven't gone up by much, and so the supply of money in their pockets hasn't gone up by much. As a result, the cost of the goods wage earners buy (such as loaves of bread and TVs) haven't gone up by much.

It's a different story for the top 5% who got most of the new money, and especially the top 0.1% which got the lion's share of the new money. The things the super-wealthy want to buy are limited in supply—luxury apartments, paintings by Old Masters, and so on—and so the price of these goods have skyrocketed because the amount of money in the pockets of the super-wealthy has increased astronomically while the supply of these scarce goods remains limited.

The other thing the wealthy spent their money on was *financial speculation*, which is *socially useless*; no new goods and services were generated, no new jobs were created and the productivity of the nation's equipment and labor didn't increase.

While conventional economists profess to being mystified by low inflation, they're ignoring what's right in front of their faces:

1. When central banks around the world digitally printed huge amounts of money between 2000 and 2015, much of this money was invested in developing nations to expand production of goods (more soybeans, cars, TVs, etc.) and services (more tech support call centers, etc.). This new money greatly expanded the supply of goods and services available to buy on the global market.

    As a result, everything produced globally remained about the same price because the supply of money in American wage earners' pockets didn't go up by much, but the supply of goods available to buy increased. This is why things manufactured overseas like TVs and clothing actually dropped in price. What didn't increase in supply by much were things that were limited, such as apartments in cities like San Francisco, slots in top-tier universities, and healthcare. Since the wealthier households had enough money to pay more for these scarce and desirable goods and services, the price of rent, university tuition, and healthcare skyrocketed, becoming unaffordable to most households.

2. Whatever new money didn't fund overseas production went into the pockets of the wealthy who already had more than enough TVs and clothing. What they wanted was assets that generated income: stocks, bonds and real estate. As a result, the price of these income-producing

assets soared. This was incredibly obvious—the S&P 500 rose from 667 to 3,500 from 2009 to 2020—yet conventional economists continue to claim there's no inflation. There has been rampant inflation, but only in the things the wealthy want: income-producing assets.

3. Some goods and services are essential; the rest are not. We need shelter, food, clean water, trash removal, education, healthcare, a judicial system, etc. We may enjoy tourist travel, fine dining and manicures, but these are not essentials; these are discretionary expenses.

    Essentials tend to be *inelastic*, meaning our need for them can drop a bit but it can't go to zero. We can cut the amount we eat and rent a smaller apartment, but we still need food and shelter. The demand for discretionary goods and services is more *elastic* - for example, people take more vacations when they have extra money in their pocket, and stop taking vacations when they're broke. So when the cost of essentials goes up, it hurts the average household much more than does an increase in discretionary things like dining out.

4. Since stagnating wages and rising prices for essentials such as rent and healthcare are political dynamite, the government agencies tasked with measuring inflation play games with the statistics to artificially maintain the illusion that inflation is low. When the government measures inflation, it lumps all these expenses into one basket, ignoring that some are essential and some are discretionary. This distorts the reality that we have to buy essentials but not discretionary goodies. If the price of essentials goes up and the price of discretionary luxuries goes down, overall inflation may appear low, but this masks the painful reality that the cost of essentials is going up, leaving less money for everything else. But if the people are told inflation is low, they're less likely to get upset when they realize the money in their pocket doesn't buy as much as it did the previous year.

I tracked the price of burritos sold by taco trucks in the San Francisco Bay Area over 20 years, and found that while the burritos remained the same (or actually got a bit smaller), the price tripled from $2.50 to $7.50. Did your wages triple in the past 20 years? Most households had very limited increases in wages. This means it takes a lot more hours of labor to buy ten burritos today than it did ten or twenty years ago.

In other words, if we compare apples to apples—the same burrito, the same one-bedroom apartment, the same healthcare insurance—we find huge increases in costs while our incomes have barely increased. This tells us inflation is much higher than the government is willing to admit. (Apples to apples comparisons in major cities have found costs have risen by about 10% every year, while the government continues to claim prices have only risen by 2% a year.)

So now we can understand why printing money and distributing it for consumption or speculation will generate inflation—because consumption and speculation don't increase the supply of goods and services available to buy.

If we increase the supply of money enormously while the supply of goods and services remains about the same, inflation is the inevitable result. This is what history teaches us: whenever governments print huge sums of new money while the supply of goods and services remains about the same, the purchasing power of the money plummets, and what once cost $2.50 now costs $7.50.

The government can keep giving everyone more and more money but every dollar buys less and less, until it doesn't buy much of anything. Thus money-printing is a *self-reinforcing feedback loop*: the more money we print, the less it buys, so we have to print even more, which further reduces what it can buy, and so on until all the money is worthless.

We can also understand the consequences of the disruption of global supply chains and geopolitical tensions, which have reduced the global supply of goods and services. This will add fuel to the inflation fire because while the supply of money is skyrocketing, the supply of globally produced goods to buy is declining.

It's very tempting to indulge in magical thinking about this very simple supply-demand dynamic. So it's not surprising that people willingly accept the notion that "governments can print as much money as they want."

While this is true, unfortunately governments can't print as much oil, bread, etc. as they want. Every dollar the central bank prints while the supply of goods and services remains the same loses purchasing power. The more money that's printed, the less it can buy. If the government continues printing more and more money, the money eventually buys next to nothing.

It is human nature to want a free lunch, and creating money out of thin air seems at first glance to be the ultimate free lunch. But once we accept the fact that money is only a *claim* on loaves of bread and not the bread itself, then we understand that printing more money does nothing but decrease the amount of real-world goods that money can buy.

An Irresistible Lure

Finally, let's consider why the temptation to print more money is so irresistible. Since the way we create and distribute money has corrupted our political system into a *pay-to-play* bidding war for government policies that benefit the few at the expense of the many, the Federal Reserve (the Fed) can't stop printing money and distributing it to financiers, corporations and Wall Street's speculators because these are the most politically and financially powerful players.

And now that the stock market has been transformed into a billboard touting economic vitality, the Fed/government can't allow it to decline. That's another reason the Fed can't stop printing enormous sums of money and handing it to Wall Street.

But since the Fed's money-printing has enriched the few at the top for so long, wealth and income inequality have now become a political problem. The top 5% own the vast majority of the nation's stocks, bonds, income real estate and businesses. The political pressure to print more money and distribute it directly to households is increasing.

So while the Fed will continue to print trillions to distribute to Wall Street, corporations and financiers, they will now also start printing trillions more to distribute as Universal Basic Income (UBI).

We now understand why money-printing that destroys the purchasing power of the dollar is inevitable. The same can be said of every major central-bank-issued currency. The pressure to print more money will increase as the system fails, and ironically the demand to print more will only increase as the money loses purchasing power. This will only accelerate the decline in purchasing power, impoverishing everyone.

Sadly, the desire for a free lunch is irrepressible, but unfortunately there really is no free lunch.

What if We Could Create our Own Money? (Actually, We Can!)

I've taken pains to explain that central banks create their own currency digitally out of thin air. They don't need to generate any goods or services to create this new money. Those who get the new money can buy assets without creating anything. They did absolutely nothing in the way of creating value to get the money. This fraud is the foundation of our financial system and our economy. As I explained, those closest to the spigot of new money can borrow it more cheaply and in much larger sums than the rest of us. This privilege gives them the power to outbid us for assets that pay interest, dividends, rent, etc. The only possible outcome of this system is that wealth becomes concentrated in the hands of the few closest to the spigot of new money.

The advantages given those with first dibs on new money is called the *Cantillon Effect*, after the 17th century economist who first described it.

Wouldn't it be great if we could all create money? In a way, we do create money when we create goods and services which can be exchanged for money, or exchanged for other goods and services (i.e. barter). When we create *value*, we are creating something that can be exchanged for money. Value flows to what's scarce and in demand, so those with something everyone wants that's scarce can command a much higher price than those selling things that few people want and are abundant.

In the 1973 Gas Crisis described in the next section, gasoline was scarce and everybody needed it, so the price went up accordingly. When oranges are in season and there's a bumper crop, the abundance tends to lower prices. When the harvest is poor and supply is limited, prices tend to go up.

When central banks create money out of thin air, they are effectively stealing a tiny slice of every existing dollar because they didn't increase the pool of goods and services. When an individual creates goods and services, they're creating value that can be exchanged for other goods and services or money. The new good or service adds to the wealth of the entire economy, while newly created central bank money only increases the wealth of those who get it first.

Imagine a money system that only creates new money when new goods and services are created. Now imagine that the money that's created doesn't go to the super-wealthy close to central banks, but to the people who created the goods and services, i.e. *those who created the value that money represents*.

That's the way money is created in the system I'm proposing: everyone who creates value—*goods and services that serve a need*—are in effect creating their own money because new money will be issued directly to them.

Such a system realigns value, money and the incentives to create value rather than speculate with fraudulently created central bank currency that only serves to make the rich richer. Note that this money isn't *borrowed into existence* the way that fractional reserve banking creates money. This new money is issued by the new system as new goods and services are created; it isn't a loan that must be paid back with interest.

The Advantages of No Debt

But what about the plucky 26-year old trying to borrow enough money to finish his first building project? The helpful bank manager and I had a problem: we couldn't prove I didn't need the money. The only strategy left was to prove I could make the payments and talk up the collateral (the half-finished house).

The manager knew what the bank's credit department wanted to see, and so he arranged my modest construction earnings as a business, and emphasized that my earnings were rising. He also had me list my living expenses (minimal, since my wife and I were living rent-free in the half-finished house and had no other debts) and detail the costs of finishing the house, to show that the loan would be enough to pay all the remaining construction costs (the labor was mostly free, of course, since my wife and I were doing the work ourselves).

There was a big difference between a conventional 30-year mortgage and the personal loan I was seeking. Unlike in a mortgage, I wouldn't have the luxury of time; I would have to pay off this personal loan in a year.

Being unable to borrow money and pay it back over 30 years meant that I would not be paying interest for the rest of my life. As we saw in the discussion of mortgages and interest rates, being debt-free would save me *the entire cost of a new house* over the 30 years of paying interest on the mortgage. Yes, I would be paying a higher rate of interest for a short-term personal loan, but the total interest I would pay was a tiny fraction of the interest paid on a 30-year mortgage.

It's ironic, isn't it? Since I was only marginally employed, I couldn't qualify for a conventional mortgage, so I had to make whatever sacrifices were necessary to finish the house without a mortgage. But not being qualified for a mortgage meant I saved *the entire cost of a new house by not paying interest for 30 years*. Not because I was so smart, but because I was so marginalized I had no other choice.

Is there a larger lesson here? It sure looks like it to me. Borrowing huge sums and paying interest is easier because it doesn't require the sacrifices and workarounds required to get it done with a modest short-term loan.

Put another way: *the not-so-rich pay interest on money created out of thin air by banks*. The less you borrow, the less interest you pay. Over time, it adds up.

But: what if money couldn't be borrowed into existence by banks? Or what if money was created out of thin air at the bottom of the heap instead of at the top of the heap? These questions only occurred to me much later, after I learned how truly one-sided our system of money really is.

Thanks to the manager's suggestions and assistance, I got the loan, the bank earned some interest, and we got the house finished. I paid off the loan, and don't remember much about it except a sense of relief. There was no cash for landscaping, but at least there was glass in the windows instead of plastic sheets flapping in the breeze.

Section Six:
Price and Profit on a Finite Planet

The global economy has two incentives: price and profit. Everyone wants the lowest price and the biggest profit for any activity or transaction. As a result of these incentives, price and profit are what's *optimized*: every part of the global system, no matter how small, is fine-tuned to reach the lowest price of production and maximize profit for the owners. On the global scale, everything that doesn't serve these two goals is ruthlessly eliminated or ignored. (Do-gooder non-profits don't change this optimization; as worthy as their efforts might be, they are background noise in the global economy.)

But is every cost included in the calculation of price and profit? Or does the system leave out the costs that might raise prices and lower profits?

What Goes Into the Price?

After experiencing all the tropical wonders we'd anticipated enjoying on the island off the coast of Thailand—lush forests, white-sand beaches and ripe fruit—the hellish wasteland we next wandered through was a completely unexpected shock. After several days of guiding us around his home island, our Thai friend and host B.K. had taken us down a dirt pathway from his mother's house, not far from the coastline.

Before reaching the shore, we emerged in a sun-blasted clearing stripped of the tropical jungle that covered the rest of the island. This eerily lifeless dead-zone was pockmarked with what looked like enormous bomb craters, huge round holes sunk deep into the earth that were partially filled with dark, stagnant water. Nothing grew in the black water, and the air was tainted with the stench of rot and death. To accidentally fall into one of these steep-sided black-water craters was the stuff of nightmares.

The scene looked like a warzone where defoliants had killed all the plant life and a B-52 bomber raid had left a broken landscape of giant craters that had filled with poisoned water.

But no, this was the consequence of global commerce maximizing profits. Our friend explained that these round ponds had been dug to raise shrimp for sale overseas. To keep bacteria and unwanted plant life at bay, each pond had been liberally dosed with antibiotics, pesticides and herbicides while a motorized circular blade kept the toxic brew aerated so the shrimp could survive. After a few harvests, the ponds were too toxic for further use and so they were simply abandoned.

I asked, "What happens to them now?" and our friend just shrugged. There was no plan to fill in the ponds or restore the landscape, and apparently no accountability for the damage done.

Is the cost of this wasteland included in the price of the bag of frozen Thai shrimp we buy at the supermarket? No. Our global economic system only prices in production costs at the *point of purchase*, i.e. the supermarket checkout. Production costs included: excavating the ponds, the labor and materials needed to raise the shrimp and then harvest and transport them to distant markets around the world. All other costs—the unknown effects of the toxic brew on the nutritional value of the shrimp, the costs of cleanup and restoration of the damaged ecosystem—were not even measured, much less included in the retail price.

The same can be said for many other commercial pursuits of maximizing profits. As an example, minerals are mined, destroying the landscape, and a thin layer of polluted soil is spread over the ravaged earth as "restoration." The enormous quantities of water needed to extract lithium for our smartphone batteries is pilfered from agricultural aquifers, destroying agriculture and rural livelihoods around the lithium mines.

All this damage is terribly expensive to remedy, and yet there's no money in the retail price for any of what economists call *external costs*, everything that is outside the production expenses.

Tobacco offers another good example. The cost of a pack of cigarettes is based not on the long-term costs of smoking but solely on the cost of packaging the tobacco into cigarettes and marketing them. A healthy profit is of course added on top of all production costs.

Let's do the cigarette math. The point-of-purchase price of smoking two packs of cigarettes a day for 20 years is about $73,000: 365 days/year X 20 years X 2 packs (14,600) X cost per pack ($5 each) equals $73,000. For one person.

But the full price of that person's 20 years of addiction to nicotine might total over $1 million in treatments for lung cancer and heart disease, and the reduction in life span and productivity of the smoker. (The costs of secondhand smoke and emotional losses of those who lose a loved one to a painful early death is difficult to assign an economic value but it is very real.)

If the full costs of the nicotine addiction were included at the point-of-purchase, each pack of cigarettes would cost about $70 ($1,000,000/14,600).

Very few people could afford a habit that costs $140 per day ($51,000 per year).

No wonder corporations are loathe to include external and lifecycle costs in their products. If the full costs were included, the products would no longer be affordable.

If the full lifecycle and external costs of the shrimp-farming and lithium mining were included in the price of the bag of shrimp and the lithium-ion batteries, the price would be much higher, perhaps prohibitively higher.

The costs don't disappear just because they're not included in the price. The costs have been dumped on those who don't have the power to pass the costs on to the companies reaping the profits and the consumers enjoying the products.

Once you've stood in the hellish landscapes left by those who scooped the profits and then left, the comfortable illusion that the retail price covers all costs is lost forever. You realize we're only paying for a fraction of the real costs of the products and services we consume. Those costs are paid by future generations and by the residents and laborers who lacked the power to pass the real costs onto the producers and consumers.

Is this a fair and sustainable way of living? No.

The problem of what we don't measure and don't include in the price is at the very heart of our global economic system: we don't measure all the costs, and we ignore what's valuable if it can't be measured in dollars. This blinds us to what's actually valuable and the real costs of our way of living.

As author Daniel Yankelovich observed in 1972 (*Corporate Priorities: A continuing study of the new demands on business*):

1. *The first step is to measure whatever can be easily measured. This is OK as far as it goes.*

2. *The second step is to disregard that which can't be easily measured or to give it an arbitrary quantitative value. This is artificial and misleading.*

3. *The third step is to presume that what can't be measured easily really isn't important. This is blindness.*

4. *The fourth step is to say that what can't be easily measured really doesn't exist. This is suicide.*

This describes the problem with measuring cost and wealth only in money: we presume that what can't be easily measured (such as external costs) isn't important, when it may actually be more important than whatever *can* be measured in dollars. Even worse, since we don't even recognize many costs, they simply don't exist in our narratives of how the world works.

Believing what can't be easily measured doesn't exist is willful blindness, and that's suicidal.

Price on a Finite Planet

Traffic is light at 4:30 in the morning. The only people on the road are those who start or end their shift in the wee hours. Everything looks eerier in the early morning hours than it does at night, especially when a light rain is misting Honolulu's streets.

Why was I up at 4:30 am? To get to the gas station, as my old VW was nearly empty. OK, but why get gas at 4:30 am? Fear: fear of not finding a station with gas. Gas stations were being drained dry, and to fill your tank you had to get in line and hope they wouldn't run out before you reached the pump. This was the Great Gas Crisis of the early 1970s, when war in the Mideast triggered an oil embargo that hit America right between the eyes. What had always been limitless and cheap—fuel—was suddenly scarce.

The fear infected everyone. No gas, no way to get to work. No work, no money. The economy was tumbling into the deepest slump since the Great Depression, and it wasn't just gas that was scarce—jobs were suddenly scarce, too, as the Gas Crisis crushed the economy.

I could get to my University classes on my old Schwinn ten-speed bicycle, but the residential construction sites where I worked were scattered around the island and not accessible by public buses. No gas, no job. No job, no money. No money, no gas.

When essentials suddenly get scarce, people start hoarding. The most famous example in Honolulu is toilet paper. Whenever a union strike threatened to shut down the docks and stop the flow of goods from the mainland, people got nervous about running out of toilet paper. So the first thing they did was drive down to the supermarket and load up on toilet paper, even if they already had a whole closet stuffed with TP. Shelves were quickly stripped of toilet paper, creating a shortage that didn't exist prior to the hoarding.

When fuel gets scarce, people hoard by topping off their tanks. As soon as they're down a quarter tank, they get nervous and get into line at a gas station to top off. This urge to keep a full tank strained an already limited supply to the breaking point, and gas stations were putting up "no gas" signs. This triggered huge lines at the stations that still had gas. The long lines and "no gas" signs triggered more fear in everyone driving by with less than a full tank, and so they joined the next queue they saw.

I had early morning classes, and I couldn't spend an hour in line anxiously hoping the station wouldn't run dry. So I got up at 4:30 am and drove to the nearest gas station. The station didn't open until 6:30 am, and I was the first on the lot. Reckoning it was against the rules to park right next to the pumps, I parked on the street and caught up on my homework, reading Shakespeare's play *Much Ado about Nothing* in the weak interior light of the VW. Around 5 am other cars pulled up next to the pumps and I quickly moved into the queue. The light was better near the pumps—the overhead light in the Bug made a Christmas bulb look like an acetylene torch, and the print in the hardbound volume of Shakespeare's plays was small--but I felt relieved I'd get the gas I needed.

The Shakespeare play was ironic, since shortages of fuel were *much ado about something important*; consumer-driven economies can't function without abundant, affordable fuels. It would have been more appropriate if I'd been assigned *The Tempest*, as the economic storm triggered by the gas crisis was laying waste to the auto and construction industries, the two canaries in the coalmine in a recession. Headlines announced 100,000 auto workers were being laid off in a single weekend, and the ripple effects were devastating industries down the supply chain.

As a tiny cog in the construction industry, I was hoping my bosses would get another project soon, because my cash was down to the few dollars in my savings. I had literally emptied the loose change in my boyhood piggy bank (a wooden house, appropriate for a starving carpenter) to pay for my previous tank of gas.

When essentials are abundant, we assume that money will always buy whatever you need. But when essentials become scarce, money is no longer enough. Sure, you can offer a neighbor $10 for a $1 roll of toilet paper, but paying exorbitant sums in a black market bidding war isn't a long-term solution to scarcity. (Not to mention the unfairness of the bidding war: the rich can easily outbid the rest of us.) And those of us in sectors hammered by the crisis had a second problem: we no longer had the income to buy essentials.

Economic theory holds that higher prices will create new supply: the toilet paper factory will add a shift to produce more TP, oil companies will pump more oil, and refineries will crank out more gasoline. But it isn't always this easy. We can't create oil out of thin air like we can create money. Printing more money doesn't magically fill empty gas tanks. All printing money does is drive the cost of a roll of TP from $1 to $10, and ensure that those closest to the money-printing spigot will have plenty of TP while the rest of us will be scrounging for whatever alternative we can find.

The other lesson from the Energy Crisis is that oil is the *master resource*, meaning *there is no substitute for abundant, affordable fuel*. This runs counter to economic theory, which holds that when one thing becomes scarce and expensive, people will buy a substitute that's still abundant and affordable. The classic example is if beef becomes too expensive, people will substitute chicken.

This theory quickly bogs down when it comes to fuel. Maybe natural gas is cheaper than gasoline, but modifying 100 million vehicles to run on natural gas and changing thousands of gas stations to stock natural gas is not easy, quick or cheap, and neither is turning natural gas into a liquid-fuel gasoline equivalent on an industrial scale.

Even swapping diesel for gasoline runs into limits, as each barrel of oil produces limited amounts of each type of fuel: jet fuel, diesel, gasoline, etc., as well as other oil products. There is no easy, quick or cheap way to turn an entire barrel of crude oil into one type of fuel.

But what about substituting electricity for oil? This runs into all sorts of other limits. Replacing 100 million internal combustion engine (ICE) vehicles with all-electric vehicles isn't easy, quick or cheap, and neither is mining and refining mountains of lithium and other costly metals needed for hundreds of millions of batteries.

Then there's the problem of *renewable or replaceable*. We talk about solar panels and windmills as *renewable energy* but since the panels and turbine parts only last 20-25 years, they're not actually renewable like a forest, they're *replaceable*—all existing panels and turbines have to be replaced every generation. (Nate Hagens introduced me to the profound difference between *renewable or replaceable*.)

Manufacturing, transporting and installing tens of millions of replacement panels and turbines is not easy, quick or cheap—and that's just replacing what already exists. If we want to add solar and wind capacity, then we need to manufacture, transport and install millions more panels and turbines, all of which will need to be replaced (and recycled) in another generation.

Twenty years goes by fast and 25 years goes by almost as fast as 20 years. Adding a few years to the life of a solar panel doesn't turn a *replaceable* into a *renewable*. (Disposing of worn-out, unrecyclable 30-foot long windmill blades is already a costly problem, and wind energy is currently less than 2% of all global energy consumed.)

All this mining, manufacturing, transporting and installing takes huge amounts of energy, and the question is: can electricity generated by panels and wind turbines substitute for oil-fuels in all the mining equipment, bulldozers, tractors, big-rig trucks, container ships, factories, tools, forges, etc. needed to make and transport all these millions of panels and turbines, and keep them maintained and operational?

The answer is no, it can't.

And what about building and maintaining all the asphalt roads and concrete docks and harbors needed to transport all these millions of panels and turbines? Will electricity substitute for all the oil-fuels being burned to build and maintain a global transport system?

Solar and wind-generated electricity is intermittent: there's no electricity being generated at night or when the wind dies down. Our economy needs gigantic amounts of energy every minute of every day, month after month, and year after year. Intermittent power doesn't cut it. But manufacturing the tens of millions of batteries needed to store intermittent power takes an enormous amount of energy itself, and batteries are also *replaceable*: they don't last forever, and recycling their components isn't easy, quick or cheap. Batteries certainly don't last anywhere near 20 years, but even if technology advances so they last 10 years, that doesn't turn a *replaceable* into a *renewable*.

Economics is a strange field. Economists try to quantify and measure things just like the real sciences (physics, etc.) they emulate, but there are all sorts of important things that economic theory doesn't even recognize, much less measure. What is measured in economics, of course, is money, which can be very misleading.

The difficulty in replacing oil is one example. Economists look at the $100 trillion in financial wealth in the U.S., and the relatively modest size of the oil industry when measured in dollars, and they declare that the price of energy no longer matters: energy is now such a small part of the economy (when measured in dollars), it's no longer a big deal.

But when you're waiting in line at a gas station at 5 in the morning, hoping there will still be some fuel left when you reach the pump, you understand the flaw in this thinking: without plenty of affordable oil, nothing else matters. You can print $10 trillion, and pile up $100 trillion in paper wealth, but no matter how much money you create out of thin air, you can't buy a substitute for oil because there is really isn't one.

That scarcity of fuel is a distant memory, as there's been a string of rabbits pulled out of the global energy hat in the four decades since the crisis.

The discoveries of new giant oil fields in the North Sea, West Africa and Alaska, improvements in deep-water drilling, fracking and enhanced recovery techniques in conventional and unconventional (shale, etc.) oil fields all boosted oil production. We're told there's enough oil and natural gas to last for hundreds of years, so shortages will never occur.

But a lot of other things have changed in the past four decades, too. A billion more people are in the middle-class, and billions more want energy-hungry scooters, cars, air-conditioning units, air travel and all the other nice things of middle-class life—all of which consume 37 billion barrels of oil a year, a number that goes up, not down, even as more solar panels and wind turbines are installed globally every year. Global demand outpaces all new alternative energy sources and discoveries of untapped oil.

There's not many rabbits being pulled out of the energy hat these days. We're discovering only one new barrel of oil (or oil equivalents such as natural gas) for every 20 barrels we consume. When a new field is discovered, it's in remote, hard-to-get locales, and it takes billions of dollars and years of effort to extract and transport the first barrel.

In the U.S., the energy sector produces about 18 million barrels a day of oil and oil equivalents, and the U.S. economy consumes around 21 million barrels. This rough match of supply and demand insulates the U.S. from global oil shocks, but this may not last long, as the recent boom in fracking is based on sinking thousands of wells whose production drops within a year or two.

There's another lesson from the 1970s gas crisis: there may be ample reserves in the ground, but geopolitics can create shortages that upend the economy. The reliable supply and affordable price of energy over the past few decades has made us complacent about the geopolitical risks that could disrupt global oil supplies. A crisis that could trigger lines at gas stations around the world seems so remote that it's like science fiction.

That's what we all thought just before the 1970s crisis sent us circling the streets looking for a gas station that still had fuel.

Then there's the problem of affordability. Fuel can be available but if it's unaffordable to most workers, the economy goes into a tailspin. We can print money with a few keystrokes, but this doesn't magically produce the oil we need at prices the average family can afford. It also doesn't stop higher prices from gutting the economy.

The problem is we've already picked all the low-hanging fruit on the global energy tree. What's left is harder to get: it's deeper and in inhospitable locales. It costs more to extract it, transport it and refine it. We can print money but that doesn't magically restock the energy tree with cheap oil and gas.

Economics is like the envious stepchild of the physical sciences, and it likes to claim that its measurements of money are as rock-solid as physics and chemistry. But there is a big difference between physical limits and financial limits. There's no limit on how much money can be digitally printed, but there are physical limits that no amount of technology or money can erase. Just as you can't get blood from a stone, you can't increase the energy density of batteries beyond the limits of the materials.

There's also a difference between what economics measures and what the physical sciences measure. Economics measures money, which is created out of thin air, and then measures the real world by the yardstick of money. The physical sciences measure the real world in ways that can't be created out of thin air.

So we have this disconnect between economics and the real world.

Economics assumes that if there's a scarcity in the real world, all we need to do is conjure up more money out of nothing and we can buy a substitute that's cheap and abundant. And if that gets scarce, then we'll buy another substitute, and so on to infinity: there will always be a cheap, abundant substitute, and all we need is to print up some more money to get it.

If you're ever waiting in line at 5 a.m. hoping to fill your gas tank, you won't need me to tell you oil is still the one essential resource for our way of life, and there are no substitutes. Even if you're driving an electric car charged by solar panels on your roof, you still depend on all the oil needed to pave the streets you drive on, mine and manufacture the batteries in your car, fuel the container ships and trains delivering the batteries, and grow the food you need to live. Oil is the foundation of our entire industrial economy, and *replaceables* won't change that.

(The electric car contains about 750 pounds of oil-based plastic—a product electricity alone cannot produce. So much for the all-electric economy.)

Economists have so far gotten away with promoting the idea that printing up another trillion dollars in the blink of an eye will magically conjure up more oil or an alternative to oil. But money can't buy what doesn't exist, or change the laws of physics.

Economists assure us there are no limits, there will always be abundant, affordable substitutes for literally everything. Their faith in the magic of money is absolute: since money is unlimited, and money can buy everything, then everything is unlimited.

But this isn't guaranteed on a finite planet. When physical limits arise, creating more money only pushes the price of a roll of toilet paper from $1 to $10. Creating more money at the top of the financial system doesn't magically push wages up so everyone can afford $10 rolls of toilet paper; it only ensures those at the top can outbid the rest of us for whatever is scarce.

If we set aside fairy tales about the magic of money and start listening to those who measure the physical world, we find a much more cautious point of view. Global supply chains are long, and in our just-in-time delivery system any disruption at critical points can cause the whole system to break down. What we assume is rock-solid only functions if everything works perfectly and fuel remains affordable to the average worker.

While scarcities appear to be *much ado about nothing* today, they could be *The Tempest* tomorrow. Printing money doesn't solve scarcities; it only increases inequality and unfairness.

What's Being Optimized?

I'd never given much thought to the tomatoes on supermarket shelves or in spaghetti sauce until I saw all the tomatoes scattered over the side of the road in a remote stretch of California's Central Valley.

It was a hot, dusty, late-summer day, and we were driving on a two-lane country road through the vast farming flatlands, heading for a rural county fair. Big flatbed trucks were hauling huge bins of freshly harvested tomatoes, and the tomatoes were piled so high that when the trucks encountered a curve in the narrow road, some of the tomatoes on the top of the pile spilled off the truck onto the pavement and gravel shoulder.

The sheer quantity of tomatoes scattered around the bend caught our attention, and I stopped to see if any hadn't been smashed to a pulp by their fall. As a longtime gardener, I reckoned the odds were low that any of the tomatoes had survived such punishment.

To my astonishment, the tomatoes were mostly undamaged. They didn't look any different than the Roma tomatoes on supermarket shelves. They weren't smashed or even bruised. After dousing one with water, I cut it into slices with my pocket knife and tasted it: not much taste. As an experiment, we gathered up a handful of the fallen tomatoes to take home and let ripen, reckoning they'd taste better in a day or two.

The tomatoes sat on our tiled kitchen counter day after day, still as firm as when I'd collected them off the gravel and still as bland. In the time that a garden-raised tomato would have rotted into a mess, these tomatoes were still unblemished and still as tasteless as damp cardboard.

It finally dawned on me that these tomatoes had been hybridized to look like a garden-raised tomato after being shipped over long distances, at the cost of garden-fresh taste. To survive handling and long truck routes to distant markets and factories, these tomatoes had been *optimized* for hardiness and durability. There's always tradeoffs in hybridization, and what had been sacrificed was taste. These tomatoes had been optimized to look good, not taste good.

Looking out at the vast landscape of bare fields, already stripped of the tomato vines, I had to wonder if the nutritional value of the fruit had been sacrificed, too. Could something that could fall off a truck and taste like damp cardboard still be as nutritious as a traditional tomato? It was an open question without any easy answer. Sometimes what's been sacrificed isn't visible.

That's the problem with *optimization*: what's been sacrificed isn't visible because the product or service has been engineered to look good on the surface. We see a shiny red tomato, but we don't see that this tomato was *optimized* to look good as an industrial product. In an industrial economy, taste is a luxury. What's profitable is produce that survives long distances with minimal losses to handling.

Still, many forms of optimization are win-win. An airliner is optimized to cruise at high altitudes at speeds of around 550 miles per hour, and what was sacrificed in engineering to optimize high-speed, efficient cruising doesn't adversely affect the bottom line or safety.

But not all optimization is win-win. Many are win-lose: those controlling the optimization win, the consumer loses. Modern appliances look nice but they're simply not as durable as previous generations. I've personally bought a once-reliable American name-brand washing machine that failed in less than a year due to defective sensors. I've bought once-reliable American name-brand range whose oven began turning on by itself randomly within two years. What's being optimized? Profits and a nice look in the showroom. What's been sacrificed is quality, safety, reliability and durability.

When it comes to how we create and distribute freshly issued money, what's being optimized is inequality, profits and debt. What's been sacrificed is *socially useful activity* and the purchasing power of wages.

As we saw earlier, creating all money at the top of the financial pyramid optimizes inequality, since those with access to cheap credit can make money with money they didn't have to earn. Similarly, skims like high-frequency trading create big profits, but they do nothing for the economy or society.

Since private banks *borrow money into existence*, our financial system optimizes debt, which means borrowers must pay interest to the banks. The bank gets the benefit of creating money out of thin air, while the rest of us have to pay interest to get any of the newly created money.

If instead we set out to optimize socially useful activity, we'll have to change the way we create and distribute money. We'd have to create money down at the bottom of the wealth-power pyramid rather than at the top, and we'll have to distribute it to those pursuing socially useful activities rather than those exploiting the financial system to maximize their profits.

We'd have to change the incentives in the system from maximizing profits by any means available (HFT trading computers, monopolies, etc.) to *improving well-being*.

Economists Abhijit Banerjee and Esther Duflo won the Nobel Prize in Economics in 2019 for their work on the mysteries of economic growth. The most basic assumption of our present economic system is that growth fixes everything and what drives growth is whatever is most profitable.

We can visualize this system as a house with a big fancy front door to the main house and a shabby narrow back door to the utility room. Our current system optimizes the idea that pushing new money through the front door to maximize growth and profits will somehow send a trickle through the back door to socially useful activity. As a result, our system goes all out to generate growth by creating trillions of dollars at the top of the wealth-power pyramid, in the hope that a few dollars will trickle down to socially useful activity.

But it turns out growth doesn't fix everything or generate socially useful activity. Pushing new money through the front door to maximize growth and profits doesn't increase anything but wealth inequality and social malaise.

After spending decades researching growth, Banerjee and Esther Duflo concluded that the way to optimize socially useful activity isn't growth or profits. **The only way to optimize socially useful activity is to invest directly in socially useful activities that boost living standards and well-being**. If we want socially useful activity, socially useful activity has to be more valuable than playing financial games like high-frequency trading. Rather than push trillions of dollars through the front door in the vain hope that a few coins end up in the utility room, the more productive approach is to push money directly through the back door to socially useful activity.

Without being fully aware of what's been sacrificed in the trade-offs, we've optimized our current financial system to make the rich richer at the expense of everyone else. Continuing to shove trillions of dollars through the front door seeking growth and profits is only accelerating wealth inequality, political discord and social decay.

This is why I say *if we don't change the way we create and distribute money, we've change nothing.*

Profit and Work

There's a gulf between the small-business employer and employee that's about the same width as the Grand Canyon. You might think it's *who gives orders and who follows orders*, but the truly monumental divide is *who has to come up with the money to make payroll on Friday.*

The employee does the work, and expects a paycheck on Friday. This is the basic contract between employer and employee: I did the work, so you pay me for the work. Where the money comes from is not my problem.

And for my contractor partner Mike and me, it *was* a problem, as there came a time when we didn't have the money for Friday's payroll. Our employees were on one side of the canyon, expecting paychecks, and we were on the other side, choked by a deepening despair.

The problem was that we were only paid when each of the houses we were building reached specific milestones—foundation poured, roof completed, and so on. We had to pay all the expenses until the project hit the next milestone, and that payment did not come instantly; the lenders took their sweet time releasing the funds. Add in the complexity of juggling a handful of new homes under construction, each in a different phase of completion, and there came a time when there was no money left in the checking account and payroll for two crews and our office manager was due the next day.

Mike and I pondered our limited options. Having taken early retirement as a police officer, Mike was no stranger to stress and situations that were, shall we say, unwelcome. Since starting the business on a shoestring, I was no stranger to gut-wrenching financial worries. Barely scraping by after paying all the bills—office rent, workers compensation, disability and unemployment insurance, and Social Security taxes, to name the big ones—was the norm. But not making payroll—*we had to make payroll.*

All our cash had long since been dumped into the business as *working capital*, the cash needed to tide us over between payments. As the business had expanded, it had outgrown our modest working capital. We'd managed to squeak through by not paying ourselves; we'd been working 60+ hour weeks for several months with no pay.

We grimly concluded there was only one way to make payroll: take cash advances on our credit cards, and not just a few hundred dollars, either, but enough to buy a new compact car in cash should we have been so inclined.

Working without pay was one thing; going into debt was far more dangerous. No matter what happened, we'd have to make those high-interest monthly payments until the debt was paid off. And when would that be? It would only be possible to do when after every last expense was paid, including our back wages, and if there was some money left over: profit.

If we lost money, we'd have to lay off our employees and close down. Every one of our employees was just as dependent on profit as we were, but they didn't worry about it because we'd always made payroll and were careful to keep the financial stresses to ourselves.

The great divide between employees and employers is *profit*. Employees don't have to worry about making a profit, while employers must make a profit or expenses will eat up their capital and the company will go broke. Employers can only take on work that's potentially profitable. There might be all kinds of useful things that could be done, but if it isn't profitable, no employer can touch it.

Maybe the community would benefit from more low-cost housing. This new affordable housing would be *socially useful*, but no business can build it unless it's profitable.

Hold on, you say; the government can do it. But where does the government get its tax revenues from? From profitable businesses that pay employees. If there are no companies making a profit, there are no employees getting paychecks and nothing to tax. So the government is just as dependent on profit as every employee.

OK, you say, but people can volunteer, and businesses can donate materials and money. Yes, people can work for free, but they need some other source of income if they're not earning a paycheck. And if businesses aren't making a profit, they can't donate anything. Even if people donate their time, everything is still dependent on profit.

Not long after we'd borrowed the money for payroll off our credit cards, one of our carpenters made a comment about all the money we must be making because we had so many homes under construction. Mike took the office keys out of his pocket, jangled them in front of the employee, and said dryly, "Here, it's yours. Payday's on Friday." The employee's jocular expression fell, for he'd glimpsed the great divide between employer and employee, perhaps for the first time.

Here we were, doing socially useful work building affordable housing, but we were at risk of going broke since the work wasn't necessarily profitable: all kinds of expenses that we couldn't control could rise, wiping out the modest profit in our original estimate. Instead of focusing on the social value of our hard work, we were consumed with permanent, gnawing financial anxiety. (Compare this to the owner of high frequency trading computers, whose only anxiety is *how many millions will I skim this week?*)

Let's take stock of profit and work.

There can be people who want to work, people who are willing to start enterprises to do socially useful work, but if the work can't turn a profit, there won't be any jobs or companies or government tax revenues.

Sure, we understand that profit motivates people to start businesses and hire employees because, as the Chinese slogan from the 1980s put it, *to get rich is glorious*. But as we saw in the chapter on money, the easiest and fastest way to get rich in our system is to skim profits from financial games rather than pursue socially useful work that could end up being unprofitable.

If we look at it this way, we end up wondering, does this current system of ours really make any sense? Since the system for now at least seems to work OK, we generally don't ask if it makes sense. We only start wondering if it makes sense when it stops working. It's only when jobs become scarce and paychecks don't cover expenses and companies go broke that we start wondering if there might be a better way to organize our way of life.

What if the driving motivation wasn't profit, but socially useful activity? What if we could pursue socially useful activity without having to worry about making a profit? This wouldn't stop people from pursuing profits, but it would open up an entirely new way of doing business and paying people to do useful work.

Conserving and Sharing the Resources of our Planet

The subtitle of this book is *Sharing the Wealth of Our Shrinking Planet*, which as I explained previously refers to the Earth's diminishing resources. That is the ultimate goal of *The Hacker's Teleology*, and to share the wealth of our *limited-resources* planet, we first need to conserve those resources, and then share them.

Let's imagine that I've just granted you a lease on a large parcel of tropical rain forest studded with valuable hardwood trees. I've given you two sets of instructions as part of the lease:

Primary Goal

Your primary goal is to maximize profits as quickly as possible, by bulldozing roads to the hardwood trees, cutting them down and hauling them out to be sawn into boards that are then transported to a distant harbor for sale in lucrative international markets.

Since there are various regulations we're supposed to follow, you're to bribe local officials to turn a blind eye on our operation, since that's much less expensive than following the regulations.

Next, clear-cut any other trees with market value, haul them out, and burn the fallen branches and whatever remains of the once-verdant forest.

Plant a fast-growing crop on the charred land with a lucrative global market value: soybeans, etc.

These operations are what you're paid to do, i.e. the source of your share of the profits.

After two harvests, the tropical soil is depleted and on its way to becoming infertile hardpan, so we abandon the devastated landscape after a token planting of sickly seedlings that will all die (a process we call *reforestation* because it sounds good) and deposit our prodigious profits in a tax-shelter offshore bank to enjoy.

Secondary Goal

The secondary goal is to preserve the local ecosystem. You won't be paid for this, of course, since there's absolutely no profit in conserving resources; there's only profit in exploiting resources.

Your first thought is, how can I accomplish both of these mutually exclusive goals? The truth is you can't; the instructions are psychotic, delusional, disconnected from reality. And what's your motivation to work on the second goal when only the first goal—exploitation—pays you?

This is our current global economy in a nutshell. On the one hand, everyone from local officials and laborers to bankers and global investors only get paid if they exploit the tropical forest as quickly and profitably as possible. This means bulldozing roads, clearcutting native trees that don't have any value in the global marketplace, burning the refuse and leaving the soil to wash away and become an infertile desert.

The tremendous waste this produces is ignored because the *system only measures production costs and profits*. Everything else—environmental damage, the loss of future production of the forest, etc.--is treated as if it doesn't exist, since it plays no part in the production process.

The long-term costs of the damage inflicted on the once-verdant forest is ignored. The animal life that once lived there, the local populace who relied on the forest for their low-impact livelihoods—they don't count. That a rare plant might have eventually yielded up a pharmaceutical compound of great worth to humanity—that's ignored, as the only thing that's measured is today's costs and profits.

At the same time, environmental organizations may be pushing governments and corporations to make some minimal effort to conserve the forest's resources. But since conservation isn't profitable, and future returns are uncertain, there is little motivation to pursue this goal. The local inhabitants are motivated, but they're poor and politically powerless. Environmental groups feel they've achieved a real victory if they persuade the government to impose some modest regulations, but the environmentalists lack the resources to monitor the actual logging and so the regulations are easily ignored.

Global corporations concerned with their image are motivated to present a public-relations show of following the regulations, but behind the PR their actual efforts are half-measures intended to look good rather than be effective.

As we concluded in the section on optimization, the only way to accomplish a goal is to explicitly align money and motivation to serve the goal. The current system claims that growth will magically solve poverty, but since growth demands the lowest cost and highest profits, it actually impoverishes the many by squandering the planet's shrinking resources to enrich the few who own the resources and the means to exploit them.

To those who control the tropical forest and the capital needed to extract the hardwood trees, the system that enriches them and leaves the forest a wasteland, destroying local livelihoods and irreplaceable ecosystems works perfectly: they got rich extracting the resources, and that's what the system optimizes. Conserving forests is time-consuming and costly, profits are slim to non-existent, so there is no motivation in the global system as it's currently configured to conserve, much less share, the shrinking resources of the planet.

If we want to conserve resources and use them wisely—doing more with the absolute minimum of resources—then we have to pay people to pursue this goal and measure all the costs, not just in the moment of production but also future costs. Hoping that a few pennies of the profits reaped by exploitation and waste will somehow trickle down to conservation efforts is as nonsensical as hoping growth that enriches the few at the top will somehow trickle down into some socially useful activities.

Hoping that a system optimized for growth, waste, profits and terribly unequal distribution of wealth will somehow conserve resources is delusional, magical thinking. The way to address poverty is to pay people directly to conserve resources and use them as sparingly as possible, regardless of the profit or lack of profit. That's the *Hacker's Teleology* of my proposed alternative system. As noted earlier, the *Hacker's Teleology* connects the dots of *values, processes and systems* because anything less won't actually change how the system operates and what it incentivizes.

Our Unsustainable System: The Affluent Own More, Waste More, Flaunt More

The recent paper *Scientists' Warning on Affluence* in the respected scientific journal *Nature* (nature.com) summarized the fundamental unsustainability of the current global system: since the affluent consume more, they waste more and cause more environmental damage. Since they own most of the system's assets, they profit from keeping it on its unsustainable path. And since they flaunt their consumption so flagrantly (the top 10% households account for almost 50% of total consumer spending), everyone below them aspires to the same lifestyle of waste and over-consumption. These aspirations to an unsustainable lifestyle increase waste and consumption, which benefits the affluent owners of assets who profit the most from higher consumption.

Each of these incentives reinforces the others: rising consumption by the affluent generates more aspirational consumption which increases debt and profits, while all this growth of consumption increases waste and environmental degradation. But since people equate more consumption with their own happiness, they are loathe to cut consumption despite the environmental damage.

As well, since affluent owners have the money and motivation to buy political influence, any governmental restrictions on consumption are watered down.

We can see how this narrative expresses specific *values*—more consumption / growth is good because it makes us happy, more growth is good because the profits trickle down to the poor, reducing poverty, and more profits are good because greed is the motivator for innovation—all support the *processes* of optimizing profits and ignoring external costs, and together the incentives and processes create an interconnected *system* that is resistant to any attempt to reduce waste, environmental damage and consumption, because this would reduce the profits flowing to the politically powerful affluent.

"Green" Energy Cannot Replace the Fossil Fuels that Enable More Consumption

The affluent few at the top constantly assure us that all their over-consumption will soon be *green* because all the dirty fossil-fuels they currently burn will be replaced by sustainable, renewable energy that will not only be endlessly abundant, it will be cheap.

None of this is remotely realistic. It is just more self-serving magical thinking.

Though we can be forgiven for thinking that printing more money creates more consumption because the money can be used to buy more stuff, consumption is tied not to how much money is printed but to how much *low-cost, high-density* energy is available. (Recall that central banks can digitally create money at zero cost, but they can't digitally create oil, grain, microprocessors, generators, etc. at zero cost.)

Energy is consumed in every layer of the global economy. It takes huge amounts of energy to smelt and forge metals, to manufacture goods, ship them around the world, pave roadways, grow and harvest food, cool buildings, and so on. The energy we consume directly as electricity in our homes and fuel in our vehicles is only a fraction of all the energy consumed.

The problem with energy is that if it becomes too expensive, 90% of consumers can no longer afford to buy as much as they did before, and the economy slumps into recession. But if the price drops too low, producers can't afford to sell energy at a loss, and so they reduce production, starving the system of the energy needed to increase consumption.

Another problem is *energy density*. To be useful, a great deal of energy must be packed into a small space. Imagine piling a small mountain of wood into your car if low-energy-density wood was the only fuel available. Imagine the heavy weight and bulky size of your mobile phone if large, low-energy density batteries replaced small, high-energy-density lithium-ion batteries. Low-density energy simply isn't that useful. Trickles of electricity generated by wind and solar must be concentrated into high-density storage such as lithium-ion batteries in order to be useful.

Another problem is the *intermittency* of energy sources such as wind and solar. The advertised energy output of intermittent sources is much higher than the actual real-world output: clouds block the sun, solar panels don't work at night, the wind dies down, etc. To be practical, intermittent energy must be backed up by sources that run 24/7. These are very expensive requirements: maintaining backup systems is costly, buying and maintaining large batteries is costly, and concentrating diffused energy into high densities is costly. And all of these systems must be manufactured, shipped and maintained at enormous expense. They will never be free.

All energy sources run down or run out. Oil wells become depleted, solar and wind systems must be replaced, and so on. Since the cheapest, easiest to extract energy is used first, eventually all that's left is the expensive, hard-to-get sources.

The magical-thinking narrative being promoted by the affluent owners of capital is that the world economy's vast consumption of oil (about 85 million barrels a day) can be painlessly replaced with "green" energy, i.e. renewables (which as we've seen are actually *replaceables*) such as wind and solar. These alternative sources currently supply about 3.3% of all energy consumed— basically background noise.

The Only Path to Sustainability Is to Cut Consumption and Distribute Power

To share the wealth of our diminishing resources, first we must conserve them by reducing over-consumption and waste. The only sustainable way to accomplish this is to distribute the power of ownership and political influence so the many have a consequential say and a stake in the system.

The movement toward a sustainable system of reduced consumption is called *Degrowth* (*decroissance* in French.) The goal of Degrowth isn't just to consume fewer resources; to reach that goal while sharing the wealth of the resources we're conserving, we must also change the ownership of financial and political power so it's no longer concentrated in the hands of the self-serving few.

Jason Hickel, author of *Less is More: How Degrowth Will Save the World*, said that *"Degrowth stands for de-colonization, de-enclosure of commons, de-commodification of public goods, de-intensification of everyday life, the de-thingification of humans and nature, and the de-escalation of ecological crisis."*

The problem is, how do we institutionalize these values in a system so that the processes yield the outcomes we desire? A great many observers write about the values, but their prescriptions for change are vague because they don't have a specific plan that integrates (i.e. connects the dots) of values, processes and systems. That's what I lay out in the next section of this book.

Section Seven:
Fairness

I first met my contractor-boss Denny's new partner Dan Moore as his carpenter-helper on a small project, building an expansive open-beam trellis over a large backyard lanai. Dan was in his fifties, tall, graying at the temples, and distinguished in manner to the point that our painter nicknamed him "The Duke." Hailing from Cajun country in Louisiana, Dan's speech was sprinkled with slight echoes of his roots, certain intonations that are unique to that culture.

Dan had been a production carpenter and contractor before moving to Honolulu, building subdivisions in the high-growth 1950s and 1960s in southern California, and I immediately noticed his many production tricks, which ranged from simple timesavers such as tying extension cords together so they wouldn't come loose when working on the roof to mastery of the heavy-duty worm-drive Skilsaw.

After we became friends, he shared his first impression of me: a skinny pony-tailed kid with a weird knack for crossing my feet and then lowering myself into a cross-legged pose.

I'd never worked with a production carpenter before and was amazed that we finished what Denny had estimated to be a multi-day job in just one day. There was no wasted motion in Dan's work flow, no errors, no chitchat. Working with Dan was a cram course in clean, fast production of the kind that separates the real pros from everyone else. There was no limit on what Dan could build; during a complicated remodel on a beachfront home, the owner wanted a small Asian-style curved bridge as a feature in the front yard. Dan cut the pieces without any plans for me to nail together. Once it was painted Chinese Red, it added a charming Asian character to the previously bland entry.

Dan and his wife Gloria invited us over for dinner, and I treated them to a movie and dinner out. Dan and Gloria also hosted the crew to watch Sunday football on TV; theirs was a relaxed, convivial household.

Looking back, it's clear that Dan was a father-figure to me, easier to relate to than my own emotionally restricted father and willing to teach me far more than I could ever learn from my workaholic white-collar Dad.

In occasional serious moments, Dan told me I'd be much farther along in the trades if I hadn't wasted all that time getting a college degree. I understood his point, which was eminently practical and undoubtedly true. But under his tutelage and guidance, I'd still managed to advance despite working only 2/3rds of the time while I finished my university studies.

One memory sticks in my mind of all the jobs I worked on as Dan's apprentice. A building supply representative came on the job, glanced at Dan and me, and then asked to see the boss. There was no way a skinny kid with a pony tail and dirty jeans was the boss, but when he assumed Dan couldn't be the boss, Dan's expression telegraphed a mix of emotions I have a hard time explaining: frustration, "here we go again" resignation and a sense of the rep's assumption being *tiresome*.

Once Island Trends expanded, Dan shifted to supervising multiple jobsites, and I joined Frank Bramlett's crew. Frank was about 15 years older than me, in his late thirties, and built like a running back. I was impressed that he could not just touch his toes but lay his palms flat on the ground, something only my hero Bruce Lee could do.

My first day on the job, what surprised and delighted me was that Frank had an astonishing Robin Williams-like sense of humor long before Robin Williams appeared on TV. Frank would take on several roles and change voices to play each part, in an endlessly inventive series of jokes and quick skits.

But even though he often had the crew laughing, he was a strict taskmaster and an exacting carpenter-builder. His father had been a contractor in Los Angeles, and so Frank knew firsthand the constant headaches, stresses and risks of the business. As a result, he'd made the decision to not become a contractor and instead earn a rewarding, far less risky living as a carpenter-foreman. He would joke with me, saying he watched the way I studied every move Denny and Dan made to learn the contracting business.

Frank could also build anything, from running a slip-form crew on a concrete high-rise to fashioning a curved staircase in the custom home we were building in the exclusive Waialae Iki neighborhood of East Honolulu.

I'd stop by Frank and his wife Mamie's house in Hawaii Kai, which was as neat and tidy as Frank's tool collection and jobsites, and listened to his life stories with keen interest, trying not to hurt myself laughing when he'd make a funny facial expression to match his jokes.

Frank was like the uncle I'd wished I'd had, someone funny, talented and world-wise who taught me so much. He wasn't afraid to share stories of his mistakes, such as building his first cabinet with 2X4 framing so it was impossibly heavy. He knew this was how to teach without appearing to teach.

Frank had a strong work ethic and strong sense of ethical conduct. When he overheard a new worker say a racial slur, apparently without even being aware that it crossed a line, Frank immediately dismissed him.

A few years later, after I'd moved to the Big Island and started our contracting business, Mamie accepted a transfer to the Big Island as a bank branch manager, and so I was able to recruit Frank to build our most complex, challenging custom homes. There were only two people I trusted with absolute confidence to get the work done right and on schedule—my close friend Steve Toma, who'd become a cabinet and furniture maker, and Frank. I was never even close to Frank's skill and experience, and now that I look back, it's amazing that I only showed up once or twice during the six month construction of our most expensive and impressive custom homes.

When I put together the paperwork Frank and Mamie needed to build their own house—plans, permit, insurance, and so on-- I was proud that I could finally do something for Frank as a token of my appreciation for his tutelage and friendship.

You may be wondering why this account of my two carpentry-builder mentors and friends leads the section on *Fairness*. Some of you might have guessed that the sales rep didn't see Dan as the boss because Dan was African-American, and that Frank dismissed the local worker because being African-American, Frank did not tolerate ethnic slurs on his jobsite.

The essence of bias is *being treated not as a unique individual but as one of a profiled group*.

I'd had a previous lesson on the complexities of bias and fairness when I was 14 and my mom and stepfather Jim took us to Detroit for the summer so he could earn a master's degree at Wayne State University.

Jim rented us a flat in a house owned by Armenian immigrants in the Highland Park neighborhood. In 1968, this was an African-American neighborhood, lock, stock and barrel. There were no Caucasians other than our Armenian landlords and their adult son. Latino, Asian and Arab residents had not yet migrated to Detroit in any significant numbers. We were the only Caucasian kids in the neighborhood.

My oldest sister Christine started working at a temp agency. My sister Connie was still too young to work. My 10-year old brother and I were worried about how we'd be treated by the neighborhood kids. Our curiosity was answered on the second day, when some boys yelled an invitation to come down and join them setting off some fire crackers. This sounded fun and the invitation seemed sincere, so we went down and lit some firecrackers. I think the neighborhood boys were as curious about us as we were about them.

Detroit had been shredded by large-scale riots the previous year, and we were naturally wary in an unfamiliar city and neighborhood where we stuck out like sore thumbs. On top of that, we were scrawny, slightly built kids. But the only sirens we heard were on the freeway a few hundred feet from our rental; the neighborhood felt unthreatening.

Soon we were walking under the freeway and the few blocks needed to reach the classic brick YMCA on Woodward Avenue. I was fascinated by the huge indoor gym with multiple basketball hoops and the wooden track that circled the gym above the court, which was tilted in the corners like a racetrack. I joined pickup basketball games with older guys, and nobody harassed or shunned me or treated me any differently as far as I could tell. If there were any other Caucasian kids around the Y, I never saw them. I went there to play hoops and run around the track, just like everyone else, and I felt accepted as just another kid who wanted to join a pick-up game. In a short time, it was normal to see African-American faces and strange to see Anglo faces.

A 14-year old Anglo outsider could never understand the experiences of the African-American residents of Highland Park. But even the 14-year old could sense the neighborhood's *social cohesion* that provided some respite from the institutional racism of the world outside. The neighborhood wasn't torn by conflicts; it felt cohesive and predictable, and I was grateful that a vulnerable outsider like me could walk to the YMCA and join some community sports in a live-and-let-live atmosphere.

I would walk past the nearby church on Sundays and hear the congregation's rousing hymns, and wish I could experience the service, obviously so much more exciting than the staid, low-key Presbyterian services I was accustomed to, but I wouldn't have dreamed of approaching the sanctuary without an invitation, out of respect as an outsider.

Let's face it, humans are prone to biased categorizations that are unfair to individuals, and human-led institutions are thus prone to treating individuals unfairly. We've now set all sorts of policies and goals to eliminate bias, but does anyone think any institution has been freed of bias because of these rules and goals? They've helped, yes, but is there some other more effective way to reduce or even eliminate bias?

If so, how do we design our alternative system to eliminate as much human bias as possible?

To answer that, let's touch on my experience with another mentor, quantitative analyst Stewart Pillette. Stew had been a stockbroker at Drexel and other big brokerage houses until he started his own small quant shop in San Francisco in his early 50s. I only worked for Stew for a year and a half from early 1997 to autumn 1998, running his back office, but during that brief period I learned a lot from him about the stock market, quantitative analysis and about being a good boss.

Stew was positive, even when things were going badly. He was enthusiastic about the market, his weekly golf, and his family. He lived his business credo: "Get it early, get it right and make a difference."

We had a complex mixed-technologies system to maintain, and snafus were constant. Market data came in via a satellite feed into a Linux box, and various processing steps required DOS and Linux line commands. When it all worked, Stew would exclaim, "I love technology!" And when it fizzled, he would exclaim with equal force, "I hate technology!"

I'd started trading stocks in early 1995, right after the Netscape browser transformed the Internet by displaying web pages written in HTML mark-up language. Stew had been selected by the *San Francisco Chronicle* as a top stock-picker and so on the off-chance he needed an assistant, I wrote him a letter.

It turned out he needed an assistant very badly, as his programmer had just quit and there was no one to collect all the data and run the programs to turn the data into useable charts--and without the charts he had nothing to sell his mutual-fund manager clients. Stew's business was falling apart.

Though Mike and I had bought three of the first Apple Macintosh computers for our contracting business in 1985, I had zero experience tinkering with the components inside PCs, typing line commands and everything else I suddenly had to learn. When one of the office PCs stopped working, the programmer guided me over the phone through opening the case and re-attaching the hard drive cables. For reasons unknown, this fixed the problem and the PC booted up. Eventually I learned enough Telnet to log into the office PC and print documents from home, write simple Linux scripts, and code HTML for Stew's first website.

As mentioned earlier, I'd long had an interest in artificial intelligence (AI) and had read numerous non-technical books on the advances in the field from as part of my research for writing my first novel, *Of Two Minds*. Even with my very limited exposure to scripts and mark-up languages, I saw that *software treats every user the same, unless the programmer specifically adds human bias.*

The best way to treat every individual equally is to automate all processes and interactions so there is no space for human bias to manifest. As for software that might express human bias either purposefully or accidentally, the answer for that is *open-source software*, in which the code is visible to all.

Given the incentives in our current system, it's unsurprising that most AI systems are focused on maximizing corporate profits by using Big Data to target individual consumers—*socially useless activity*, akin to HFT trading systems—or for surveillance and control by governments or corporations, a *socially negative activity*.

This leads us to ask: what if AI was focused on eliminating human bias by automating our alternative system to pay people to do *socially useful work*? What if the purpose of AI software wasn't to maximize corporate profits or government control but to ensure fairness by treating every individual in exactly the same way? Wouldn't this be the truly worthy goal for AI?

Section Eight:
A Sustainable Alternative

We've finally reached the point in this book where we can connect all the dots of my experiences and what we've learned about belonging, getting ahead, workarounds, systems and money into a new alternative system which I call the *Community Labor Integrated Money Economy* (CLIME), the end result of my *hacker's teleology* connecting the dots of *values, processes and systems*.

As noted earlier, those proposing alternatives to the current arrangement focus only on values, not processes or systems that integrate incentives and processes. In this they are like Marx's vague, ungrounded descriptions of a socialist utopia: inspirational but misleading. The hard part is integrating processes and feedback loops into a system that manifests the desired results *as the only possible output of the system*. That's what CLIME does.

The Experiential Roots of the New Arrangement

In my experience, the roots of my proposed CLIME system are pretty clear. Belonging, getting ahead, accomplishing work that makes a difference, achieving mastery, fulfilling one's ambitions, finding ways to express one's enthusiasms, belonging to something that reflects the values of fairness and sustainability—these are the essential lessons of my life.

Belonging to something that is purposeful, meaningful and larger than oneself is a core human need—perhaps the primary human need beyond the physical basics of survival. We want to be treated fairly, so that *equal effort brings equal respect and equal rewards.*

We want to expand our horizons and our identity. We want an opportunity to excel and gain mastery, to get ahead in the world and to fulfill our ambitions via *gainful employment*. We want a chance to find mentors who see our potential and who can help us fulfill that potential. We want access to an *economic ecosystem* where the tools, human and social capital and markets we need are available to every member.

The status quo offers no path to an organized, productive belonging that guarantees gainful employment and a way to get ahead. Belonging, a livelihood and an opportunity to get ahead are all hit-or-miss in the current arrangement. Maybe you get an opportunity, maybe not. Maybe you get treated fairly, maybe not.

In our current system, a pathway to experiencing the *rightness of being true to ourselves* is also hit-or-miss, especially for unconventional misfits like me. A pathway to mastery of operational and hands-on skills is equally as haphazard.

The status quo solution is what's known as *Universal Basic Income*, which results in no path to belonging, being useful and valued, earning dignity and a livelihood, a way to get ahead—nothing but just enough money to barely get by, money which is increasingly prone to losing purchasing power. It is like paying a lonely kid to shoot baskets alone.

Any new arrangement can't be a top-down, easily corrupted hierarchy like all the institutions in our current arrangement. Instead it must be self-organizing, adaptive, flexible, i.e. designed to promote workarounds and reinventing ourselves. In other words, it must be a *loosely bound* system with multiple pathways connecting every participant to the flow of knowledge, capital, goods and services. It must be a network, not a pyramid in which orders and authority trickle down from the elite at the top.

This new structure must be rich in feedback loops between members in each group, and between groups. Being dynamic, it may be messy, even chaotic at times, in a low-level hum of variability like a natural ecosystem. It must be anti-fragile, becoming stronger with every challenge and crisis.

The rules governing such a network must be instantiated in software that treats every member and every group equally. In other words, the rules governing the system must manifest a standard set of core values where everyone is treated equally, everyone has a say, everyone is rewarded fairly for equal effort and responsibility, and everyone has an opportunity to take a leadership role. Cheating or shirking (known as *free-riding* on the efforts of others), abusing the authority of leadership, and failing to treat everyone equally must be grounds for dismissal and revocation of the privileges of membership.

In other words, this arrangement must be both an *economically purposeful* system that is productive in the real world and an *internal values system* that develops the core values of equal voice, effort, reward and responsibility, treating everyone fairly and offering equal opportunities to get ahead. (Opportunities to get ahead can be equal but outcomes cannot be guaranteed. How the dots of each individual's life connect up is as unique as each individual.)

These new values are very basic: play your best, but play for the team. Teamwork requires some sacrifice. This will be made clear when we join the team, and in a way, we want to make sacrifices because this is an essential part of earning respect and dignity.

This arrangement must have its own system of money that it controls lock, stock and barrel. To ensure that the money cannot be distributed to an elite at the top as in the current system, this money can only be created at the lowest level of the organization, *by the labor of individual members*.

This new system's money would be a *labor-backed cryptocurrency*, created out of thin air like central bank money, but unlike central bank money, it won't get created by the few to exploit the many. It will be limited because the labor of members is limited, and since it is a cryptocurrency it cannot be counterfeited.

Since the labor of individuals working in groups generates goods and services, the expansion of the supply of money and the supply of goods and services will be in a natural equilibrium. As a result, the destabilizing imbalances between the supply of central bank money and the supply of goods and services that currently create inflation cannot arise and impoverish everyone.

And since there is no mechanism in the new system to digitally print unlimited money and distribute it to elites, this new system of money cannot generate the destabilizing inequality that is the natural result of our central bank system of money, an inequality that has corrupted our society.

Rather than establish monopolies to maximize profits, this new arrangement will optimize transparent trade in goods, services, capital and knowledge. Creating a surplus that can be traded with other groups will be encouraged, as well as friendly competition.

In the new system, cooperation and competition are not *either-or*; they are two sides of the same coin. Competition will drive the productive desire to excel, while cooperation will provide the tools and capital of an economic ecosystem that every group can use. Everyone will be exposed to the same risks of projects not working out as anticipated. Unlike our current financial arrangement, the new system will have no mechanism for an elite to transfer risk to others.

In this new system, money will be created and distributed for producing *socially useful goods and services*. There will be no way to create and distribute money for all the *socially useless, parasitic activity* that is the primary source of profits in our current financial system.

Since profit will no longer be the sole means of *assessing what's valuable* in this system, this new arrangement will also provide a way to pay people to do valuable, important work that is totally, completely unprofitable, for example, restoring habitats destroyed by profit-maximizing corporations and governments.

Broadening the work that can be paid to include everything that is valuable but not profitable is the only way humanity can reduce the burdens being placed on the planet's resources by the current arrangement's monomaniacal obsession with *over-consumption at any cost* and *maximizing profits by any means available.*

What's being optimized in the new arrangement is *sharing the wealth of a shrinking planet*, i.e. sharing the limited resources and habitats of Earth. What's optimized *is doing more with less* (i.e. Degrowth). What's optimized is reducing the systemic inequality and unfairness that is destroying the planet to enrich the few while impoverishing everyone else.

Since we respond to price, the new arrangement will have mechanisms for including all the *external costs* left out of price in the current system: all the environmental damage, the unhealthy consequences, and the social costs of consumption. Rather than act as if not measuring these costs means they don't exist, this new arrangement will recognize that measuring what is real is essential to making wise decisions about allocating labor, capital and resources. We've blinded ourselves by refusing to measure real costs and as a result humanity has blundered into catastrophically bad decisions.

Burnout: If the Status Quo Can't be Seen as Failing, then Only Individuals Can Fail

There's one important experience that I haven't described yet that fundamentally influenced my design of CLIME: my experiences with severe burnout. In the section "Workarounds and Reinventing Ourselves" I mentioned that I'd burned out after five years of building dozens of homes, a commercial project and a subdivision, and was lost and depressed enough to seek professional help.

Severe burnout is one of those things that only those who experience it can understand. If you haven't burned out, you can't really grasp the severity of it. Yes, it's mental and physical exhaustion, and profound depression. But it's much more than exhaustion and depression, both of which have conventional cures: just take it easy for a few weeks and start anti-depressant medications and cognitive therapy, etc. But these conventional therapeutic responses don't actually cure burnout, though they might alleviate the severity of the symptoms.

Burnout is deeper and more profound than exhaustion or even depression. In the depths of severe burnout, you lose your willpower, your ability to force yourself to keep juggling all your responsibilities. You collapse under the load, much like a beast of burden who reaches its absolute limits, and you no longer have the strength to care. You're not just mentally and physically exhausted, you're emotionally drained to the point of feeling very little beyond exhaustion.

Burnout is not well understood because it hasn't been studied much, since it's not considered a condition with a defined diagnosis like depression or anxiety disorder. However, some of the few studies that have been done have found that the brain is altered by burnout, and recovery can take several years. My experience was that my mind no longer worked effectively, with lapses of memory and cognitive function that never happened before I burned out.

Burnout is an internal experience with few if any physical symptoms that can be measured. Blood pressure, cholesterol, etc., typically remain normal despite the collapse of the burnout's mental and physical energy. Given our medical system's reliance on tests for diagnosis and *standards of care* for treatment, burnout is viewed as an individual's psychological condition rather than as a manifestation of our socio-economic system.

Our medical system also tends to separate psychological problems from physical ailments. But burnout is a whole-being experience: it is a mental, psychological, physical, emotional, and at least in my view, spiritual collapse.

In pondering my own experience, I've concluded that a strictly therapeutic perspective—here's an individual who burned out, how do we alleviate their suffering and aid their recovery—doesn't reflect the experience or the causes.

Part of the difficulty in understanding burnout is that individuals don't respond to overwhelming pressures in a uniform way. Some people seem incapable of burning out, while others experience recurring bouts of burnout or may even experience a complete collapse that takes months or years to recover from.

Surveys suggest that the more the individual demands of themselves (what some might consider *perfectionism* or *obsessive-compulsive* behavior), the greater the likelihood they will burn out as their responsibilities increase. There are undoubtedly other shared traits in those more likely to burn out than those who seem impervious to it.

But I think there are systemic factors in burnout that have little to do with the individual's psychology and everything to do with the way our economy and society are structured. There's a contradiction between what we're told will lead to success and what we actually experience.

These socio-economic causes are ignored, as the system is presumed to be either ideal or the only possible way to organize civilization. Since the system can't be seen as failing, all failure is viewed as an individual's failure.

In other words, failure is an individual's problem; *we fail the system*. But perhaps it's actually the other way around: maybe *our socio-economic system is failing us*.

In my view there are four systemic dynamics in burnout.

1. Risk is not apportioned fairly in our economy.

Those who make money with low-risk financier tricks such as high-frequency trading have limited risk of personal losses. Borrowing cheaply from the central bank and buying Treasury bonds is effectively zero-risk. Certainly there is no physical risk in these activities compared to construction, mining, etc. *Socially useless parasitic profiteering* is clean and safe.

Compare that to small businesses exposed to personal losses, where the owner must personally guarantee loans, and any lawsuits target the owner directly. Actual production work comes with physical risks of injury. (I'll resist the temptation to list all my injuries and near-misses; disabling injuries, potentially crippling falls, etc. sound so melodramatic.)

All these risks are open-ended, meaning it's impossible to limit the risks of being slapped with a frivolous lawsuit, a regulatory audit, the sudden emergence of a corporate competitor or a slowing economy. Open-ended risks generate open-ended stress.

In classical capitalism, risk and return are linked: to earn outsized profits, the entrepreneur must accept outsized risks. For example, to reap the enormous gains from selling spices harvested in Indonesia in 17th century Europe, a trader would have to pay for a ship and crew and put up the money to buy the spices once the ship reached its destination half a world away.

If the ship sank in a storm—not an uncommon occurrence--all would be lost. A trader could buy some insurance, but that would not replace the losses. The risks weighing on the crew were even higher—death from disease, shipwreck, piracy, etc.

Small businesses come with risks, many of which are open-ended: there isn't any insurance that will cover all financial and work-related stresses, and potential gains are generally modest. Compare these open-ended risks to the low-risk, essentially guaranteed returns in high-frequency trading and similar strategies available to financiers. In our current system, risk and return are only linked for those at the bottom. For the few at the top, risk has vanished. They can reap enormous gains without having to take any risk at all.

This inherent unfairness and imbalance has fatally distorted the system. Those at the top reaping the benefits reckon that *since the system works for me, it works for everyone*, but this is not true. *The system only works for those at the top.*

2. There's an unbridgeable gulf between what we're told leads to success and the real-world results of "doing all the right things."

Historian Peter Turchin explained that economic declines are characterized by three conditions: a surplus of entitled elites (what Turchin calls "overproduction of parasitic elites"), stagnation of wages, and a decay in public finances. All three are now clearly visible. There simply aren't enough elite slots offering secure pay, high social status, etc. for the millions of aspirants with advanced degrees, family connections, etc.—advantages that would have guaranteed an elite slot a generation or two ago.

Conventional wages have been stagnating or decades. Adjusted for inflation, wages have stagnated since the 1970s, and since 2000 even in the top tiers of employment. On top of the stagnation in purchasing power, wages and benefits are increasingly insecure—here today, gone tomorrow.

It's apparent that following the conventional path doesn't necessarily lead to success. Instead, the costs are now so great and the system so fragile that burnout is increasingly the result.

Public finances were precariously dependent on debt before the pandemic, and now the explosion of debt is rapidly increasing the fragility of public finances globally.

Longtime readers know that I've focused considerable attention on scarcity being the source of value and on the difference between *tradeable* and *untradeable* labor. Digital editing of a video can be done anywhere on the planet, so it's tradable. Welding a boat trailer or installing a roof vent must be done locally, so it's untradeable. In a globalized, digitized economy, labor that's tradable is unlikely to be scarce (and thus is less valuable). Credentials such as college diplomas that were once scarce and therefore valuable are now common so of little value.

If we consider these structural realities, it's clear that following the conventional path no longer leads to the promised success. Put simply, the system is failing us, not the other way around.

3. The assumption that our system has room for everyone to succeed if they follow the conventional path is contradicted by our real-world experience.

This contradiction creates an inner disconnect between *what we experience* and *what we're told we should be experiencing*. Our inability to reconcile this contradiction manifests in a host of disorders: poor diet and health habits, difficulty sleeping, lack of engagement with real life, inability to maintain meaningful relationships, reliance on medications, addictions to drugs/social media, etc., inability to concentrate, frustration, depression, anxiety disorders, and so on. All of these are manifestations of chronic stress which have been *normalized* to the point that we accept inhumane working conditions as "normal."

For example, we're now expected to respond to work messages at all hours of the day and night, endure soul-deadening commutes and impossible workloads, and also manage the stresses of financial insecurity and declining health, all without noticing or even feeling the insanity and destructiveness of it all.

In effect, our experience is *de-realized*: what we experience and feel must not be real because it's so at odds with what we're supposed to be feeling. The gulf between what the system demands of us as *economic units* and what we're able to give widens to the point where we simply can't go on and we collapse into burnout.

Just why does our current system make these obviously insane and destructive demands of us? Because every economic activity must reap an outsized profit for someone somewhere, and the system must push over-consumption (and the debt to pay for it) to new heights or the system will collapse.

As noted earlier, what our current system measures is GDP—growth, in financial metrics. Everything else—the sustainability of the system, the external costs, the *livability of the system*—are not measured. Since they're not measured, they are treated as if they don't exist.

Economist Joseph Stiglitz and others have long recommended that we change what we measure and optimize, since relying on GDP/growth as our measure of prosperity has severely distorted the global economy.

What nobody seems willing to admit is the system we live in generates burnout as a consequence of the pressures placed on individuals to maximize profits and over-consumption, regardless of the destruction these wreak on the planet and the humans ensnared in the system.

The implicit assumption is that there is simply no other way to organize an economy and society other than this insane, destructive arrangement. But this is clearly false; there are many other ways to organize civilization.

Since we're told the system is working great even as our experience tells us it's failing, we internalize the contradictions and try to compensate for the system failing us. We think our own sound eating and fitness habits, strong work ethic and high ethical standards will see us through, but we're wrong; individuals have limits while the system's demands on us are limitless.

Experiments with rats reflect the realities of living in a failing system. Like humans, rats are social animals, with hierarchies of status and complex bonds within groups. When rats are crowded into a space without enough room for every individual to have a positive social role, the social structure and individuals' ability to cope both break down. Individual rats either withdraw into extreme isolation and passivity or they become hyper-aggressive, competing for one of the few positive social slots at the top of the social pyramid.

Japan's economy has been failing to offer positive roles for all its workforce for decades, and so it's not surprising to find that many young people have withdrawn from the economy and society, holing up in their rooms at home. This social disorder is widespread enough to have its own name: *hikikomori*, literally *pulling inward*, in a form of acute social withdrawal.

This withdrawal and isolation is increasingly visible in America and elsewhere, too, as rates of depression, suicide and withdrawal in the young continue to rise. The is the result of our current system's failure being *normalized* and our individual experiences of this failure being *de-realized*, i.e. treated as an individual's aberrant psychological condition rather than as a manifestation of systemic failure.

4. Meeting all the expectations of the current system requires abandoning our true selves for a superficial mask of compliance.

The 19th century Danish philosopher Soren Kierkegaard placed the individuals' *acquisition of oneself* as the goal of human life. When we set ourselves aside to meet others' expectations, we're wearing masks, i.e. not being truly ourselves. In Kierkegaard's view, this is not only a psychological conflict, it is also a profoundly spiritual one. This is also my view, one that Kierkegaard helped me understand.

That everyday life in our system is a spiritual crisis with no resolution is a taboo that is defended by ridicule and denial. Since the system can't be seen as failing, then only individuals can fail. If we break down, it must be our own fault, and the system has nothing to do with it.

But the reality is our system has failed us, although those benefiting from the unfair distribution of wealth use all their power to deny this reality.

Burnout strips away our conventional "do what the system demands" masks and forces us to confront the contradictions and destructiveness of the system. Everything that was de-realized eventually becomes clear, and we realize that we must place the acquisition of ourselves above the conventions of passive compliance.

From this place of awareness, the question arises: why can't there be an alternative system that allows us to be ourselves and have a productive, positive role in society?

CLIME is my answer to this question.

CLIME as a Template for the Community Economy

One way to understand the *Community Labor Integrated Money Economy* (CLIME) system is that it's an automated template for a *community economy*, a self-organizing economic ecosystem that serves the needs and scarcities of each community, whether filling those needs is profitable or not.

The problem for anyone trying to address scarcities in their community is two-fold: (1) starting and operating an organization is difficult and requires expertise few have, and (2) funding the new organization usually requires getting grants from non-profit organizations or local government agencies.

CLIME solves both of these problems. In CLIME, the templates for starting and operating a democratically run community group are automated in software that anyone with a computer, tablet or smartphone could access. Since CLIME issues its own cryptocurrency, it is *self-funding*. Any group that completes the initial templates and gets approval for their project by the automated software will start getting paid for the work they complete every week: if you do the work, verify the work with evidence, then digital payments will be made to each members' account.

The templates ensure compliance with CLIME's values, processes and goals. The group's projects must address verifiable local needs or scarcities; no group can deny membership to a CLIME member who is in good standing; no information may be collected on members other than their name, their CLIME ID, and their CLIME work record; each group will have a democratic structure that rotates leadership roles to every member who is willing to accept a leadership position; all CLIME software will be open-source, and so on—basic rules based on the ten points listed in the following section.

Beyond these basic, common-sense rules, there will be great flexibility in CLIME groups and projects. Groups can choose to stay small and specialized, or expand into groups large enough to handle multiple projects. Groups can form alliances to complete major projects. Groups can select projects that are essentially permanent, such as child and elderly care, or they can choose projects which are one-time activities.

Individuals can be members in more than one group, working part-time for two or three groups. Members can:

- set their own availability and hours
- work in the conventional economy as well as in a CLIME group
- have a side business producing goods or services that they can sell to other members.

CLIME groups buy and sell the goods and services they produce within the CLIME marketplace, and are free to sell any surplus goods in the conventional economy. (Recall that the wages paid for completed work are created out of thin air by the software managing CLIME's own cryptocurrency. All the money in the system is cryptocurrency created to pay members for their labor. Once it's created and paid as wages, members can spend it, save it, etc., as they see fit, and groups can sell their surplus production to other groups or members.)

Groups that have served their purpose or lost all their members can be disbanded; groups will arise and prosper and some will fade away, much like enterprises in the conventional economy.

CLIME has no central leadership, so groups are self-organizing. The automated software reviews and approves projects and issues wages.

If this strikes you as impossible, consider that Amazon currently hires new workers in a completely automated process. There are no person-to-person interviews. The applicant fills out the forms online, the software processes the application, and if it's approved, instructs the new employee where to go to pick up an employee badge and start work.

The core functions of enormous systems such as PayPal, eBay, Amazon, Google, banks, etc. are already automated. Much of what we consider essential services is already automated. CLIME will not require any new technology, it will simply apply existing technology to new values and processes.

All of the rules will be instantiated in the templates for starting and operating a CLIME group. These templates will be operated by five software modules which form the AI engine of CLIME.

CLIME's Five Automated Modules

CLIME will be run on a day-to-day basis by five automated software systems which work together in an interface that's seamless to the user. I described these modules in detail in my previous book, *A Radically Beneficial World*. Since this new book is about connecting the dots of my experiences to the CLIME system, I'll only provide a basic sketch of the modules here.

The fundamental structure of CLIME is that paid jobs and equal treatment of all members must be *the only possible output of the five software modules*. In other words, there can't be any way for an elite to hijack the system for its exclusive benefit or for one set of members to exploit or oppress any other set of members.

- Module 1: The community organization: groups, membership, privileges, rules.
- Module 2: Peer-to-peer accreditation/verification: trust/accuracy/reliability ranking.
- Module 3: Cryptocurrency issuance, distribution and management.
- Module 4: The CLIME marketplace for goods and services produced by groups and individual members.
- Module 5: Transaction clearing-house for the CLIME cryptocurrency (what I call the *Largent*).

The key feature of these interlocking software engines is that they are automated to eliminate human bias and lower the cost of operation. A slow, deliberate appeals process will be available to contest automated decisions, but the basic incentive is: follow the templates and rules and you'll get approved for projects and payments. Attempting to game the system or free-ride on the work of others means you'll lose the privileges of membership. (Recall that membership is not a right; it is a privilege which must constantly be earned.)

Module 1 is self-explanatory: this software engine will maintain a database of all group activities and members, providing step-by-step templates for complying with CLIME rules.

Module 2 will manage the *reputation engine* of the system. Trust is the heart of CLIME: members must trust the system will be fair, and that they will be treated fairly by the software and other members.

To maintain trust, CLIME will follow the dictum *trust but verify*. Every group and member will be presumed to be trustworthy, i.e. each will be trusted to accurately report work completed and hours worked, reliably perform the work that the group proposed, and provide goods and services as agreed upon—but each of these activities and transactions must be verified by evidence and by other members in good standing acting as anonymous auditors.

CLIME will collect no data on members other than their name, their CLIME ID, and their work/pay/verification data. All members deserve to know the reputation ranking of other members. If a member reports inaccurate or false work records, fails to perform work they claim for payment, provides lesser goods and services than agreed upon, etc., their ranking reflects this lack of accuracy, reliability and trust.

Anyone who cheats the system cheats every member.

Since membership is a privilege, not a right, CLIME has zero tolerance for scammers, cheaters, free-riders, fraudsters or sociopaths seeking power to exploit others. Those seeking to abuse the system and their fellow members will lose the privileges of membership. (After a waiting period, they can re-apply; their low reputation ranking can only be raised by a history of compliance.)

Module 3 is also self-explanatory. Unlike other cryptocurrencies such as bitcoin that are issued as payment for maintaining the blockchain, the CLIME currency will be issued only for labor completed on an approved project by members in good standing. (A modest tax on all CLIME wages will cover the costs of maintaining the software modules and databases. The model here is open-source software such as Mozilla, which recruits users with the requisite expertise to maintain and update the software.) This module will keep track of all claims for wages, verification that the work was performed and the payments issued to each member.

Module 4 will handle the CLIME marketplace for goods and services offered by CLIME groups and members. This marketplace includes all groups and members globally.

Module 5 will handle all members' accounts, much like a bank, and all CLIME cryptocurrency transactions with other currencies, for example, taxes paid to national governments, purchases made by CLIME groups and members in the conventional economy, and so on.

While the clearing-house won't issue loans, members and groups will be able to transact peer-to-peer lending: a group or member will be able to offer interest to borrow a sum from other groups/members. All such peer-to-peer lending will be voluntary and subject to basic common-sense rules.

To keep the interface simple for members, the software will have to be complex. There is no easy way to codify such a complicated system or maintain its integrity and trustworthiness. The CLIME system will be a monumental AI undertaking that will require constant improvements and creative solutions.

A System for Sharing the Wealth of Our Shrinking Planet

As we've seen, expecting the current system to conserve resources and share the planet's wealth is like expecting a bulldozer to magically recreate the pristine forest it just destroyed. The system's only priority is *endless growth at any cost*.

The current system claims our survival depends on expanding consumption; were over-consumption to falter, the debt-based financial system will collapse and take us with it. It boils down to: *we must consume more and borrow more or the system will die*.

What will die was always unsustainable. The current system's sustainability was always an illusion, an illusion promoted by the few who benefited the most from persuading us their dominance was permanent.

Shutting Down the Old System

So how do we turn off the blindly destructive bulldozer of the current system?

First, we replace its values—that the only things that matter are growth and profits—with a system that values conservation, sustainability and *doing more with less*. How do we do this? We start with the way money is created and distributed. Where the current system values the privileges of central banking of all else, CLIME values the distribution of money to those creating goods and services that serve their community—those being productive rather than those enriching themselves via socially useless profiteering.

How does an alternate system incentivize doing more with less? CLIME will do so in two ways. One is that it will be a distribution network for *appropriate technology*, a term that covers small-scale, inexpensive technologies that can be locally produced with local materials or materials that are durable and long-lasting—the opposite of the *planned obsolescence / Landfill Economy* of the current system.

(Since it's profitable to force consumers to constantly replace appliances, etc., these are designed to fail and be difficult to repair. This *planned obsolescence* creates what my colleague Bart Dessart calls the *Landfill Economy,* as all the obsolete, broken junk generated by *growth* ends up in the landfill.)

As an example, it's been estimated that replacing traditional inefficient wood cookstoves with clean-burning, efficient cookstoves would cut wood consumption by millions of metric tons. Another example is small systems that use direct-current (DC) from a solar panel to power lighting and other uses in regions with no centralized electricity grid.

Secondly, local residents commonly have a strong self-interest in conserving the ecosystem they depend on. Once they have an income source that's not market-dependent and access to appropriate technologies that have worked well in similar environments, they will have the money and tools needed to improve their well-being and the well-being of the ecosystem they depend on for food and fuel.

For example, local cooperatives near Veracruz, Mexico have adopted low-cost *best biomass practices* to increase the wood grown on their farm plots while simultaneously reducing their consumption of wood fuel by switching to clean cookstoves. They've also planted thousands of native trees in a reforestation of former forest lands that had been cleared for pasture.

By freeing local community economies from the tyranny of global market forces imposed by corporations and corrupt governments, CLIME will not only ensure that doing productive work will earn wages regardless of the profitability of the projects, it will also give local communities the capital to buy their own tools and provide the small-scale, low-cost technologies that can make incremental improvements in the well-being of the residents and the ecosystems they inhabit.

The best way to share the wealth of our over-burdened planet is to ensure those filling the needs of their local community will get paid for their work and provide them with low-cost, durable tools and technologies that they can leverage to *do more with less—much less*. This is the essence of Degrowth: improving human well-being and restoring the biosphere while consuming far fewer resources and avoiding the ever-greater waste of the endless-growth *Landfill Economy*.

Ten-Point Outline of CLIME

Here is my ten-point outline of CLIME:

1. The opportunity to belong to a group accomplishing *socially useful activity* and be paid for one's work in the group is available to all.
2. Membership is voluntary and a privilege, not a right.
3. The groups are *self-organizing*, meaning anyone can join a group or leave a group or start a group, as long as they follow the rules of conduct. Those who refuse to follow the rules will forfeit their membership.

4. Each group is managed democratically; every member has a say, and leadership positions rotate among all members.

5. Everyone contributing to a group's work is paid with a cryptocurrency that is only issued to individual members; there is no other mechanism for creating this currency other than labor, i.e. performing work in a CLIME group. Thus it is a *labor-backed cryptocurrency.*

6. The system can only be fair and productive if its money is fair and productive, and so the system must have its own unique currency that the system issues, distributes and controls.

7. The operational tasks of each group are handled by software that treats every individual member and every group equally.

8. Socially useful activity addresses scarcities and needs in the community, a process that produces economic value in the community and the larger economy.

9. The groups are cooperative, collaborative, and in friendly competition. The global network of groups shares information, ideas, best practices and appropriate technologies and trade goods and services. These exchanges are transparent and open source; any member can look at the software code. This network of groups does not replace government or the existing for-profit marketplace; it is independent of these systems but complementary to them. The network of groups performs valuable work that governments and profit-maximizing corporations can't (or won't) do.

10. Membership is opt-in (voluntary) and flexible. Members can belong to more than one group, work part-time in a group while working for themselves in a home business, etc.

CLIME: Community Owned and Run Corporations

Since outlining the CLIME system in *A Radically Beneficial World*, I've struggled to find a way to describe its community economy and labor-backed cryptocurrency in terms that most people can grasp. The first response of many is to dismiss CLIME as too idealistic to function in the real world.

My reaction to this is: *nobody says corporations are too idealistic to function in the real world, yet CLIME groups are basically community owned and run corporations.*

Let's break down why corporations function so effectively.

They're voluntary. Nobody's forced to start / incorporate an enterprise. Nobody's forced to become an employee, supplier or customer. Everyone chooses to participate to further their own interests.

Corporations have a defined structure but are free to pursue just about any project. This structure institutionalizes a hierarchy of accountability and oversight.

Corporations have a single goal: maximize profits by any means available. This goal provides the purpose and organizing principle for everyone in the corporation.

CLIME groups have the exact same fundamental characteristics. They are voluntary, institutionalize a structure of accountability and oversight, and have an organizing principle: address the needs and scarcities of the community.

The only difference is corporations are owned by individuals, many of whom are investors, while CLIME groups are owned by the participants (members) in the community. There is no "ownership" that can be sold or transferred to outside investors. Other than this legal difference in ownership, a CLIME group is the equivalent of a corporation.

The other difference is CLIME solves the problem inherent with profit-maximizing corporations. When corporations become monopolies, i.e. they gain control of supply and markets and use this control to increase profits at the expense of employees, suppliers and customers, they become exploitive. As we've seen, the most reliable way to become highly profitable is to establish a monopoly or shared monopoly (cartel).

This is a fundamental difference between the corporate dominated marketplace and the CLIME marketplace: the CLIME marketplace is protected from exploitation by monopolies. There is no way for an elite or corporation to gain control of CLIME's currency, its marketplace or groups.

CLIME's community corporations institutionalize free enterprise, meaning participants, the community corporations and customers all have choices on how best to get ahead.

Why Doesn't the Government Do This?

The question that comes to many minds is: okay, you've made a strong case for a new system connecting work, value and community. But why can't the government do all this? After all, it already exists and it already employs tens of millions of people and has its own money system. Can't we just add some new programs to the government?

I think you know my answer: those benefiting from the current systems of money and governance will never allow the processes to change because this might threaten their share of the government's river of money.

To repeat: *if we don't change a system's values and processes, then we haven't changed anything.* More pointedly, *if we don't change the way money is created and distributed, we haven't changed anything.* Adding another program to the existing system is just like adding another layer of oversight to a corrupt tax collection system: it doesn't change anything, it only adds more complexity and more opportunities for corruption.

In terms of systems, *the government is the wrong type of system,* because it is a centralized hierarchy, i.e. a pyramid with the wealth and power concentrated at the very top. It can never be self-organizing or anti-fragile— two core requirements of the system I'm proposing.

Another problem is the government is intrinsically political, meaning that the core process of government is people advocating for their share of the pie, a process of horse-trading that manifests their biases and privileges. In other words, it's intrinsically unfair because political battles end up producing winners and losers.

As we've seen in gory detail, our government's way of creating and distributing money is inherently unfair, and it corrupts democracy via lobbying and pay-to-play campaign contributions. Since the government depends on a money system that enriches the few at the expense of the many, the economy and society inevitably manifest this unfair and exploitive foundation. To borrow a tech phrase: *garbage in, garbage out.*

We know it's not possible to have a corrupting, exploitive and fundamentally unfair financial system and a fair, productive, just and democratic society. If you want a fair and just society, then you must start with a fair and just financial system.

And finally, the government is like the rest of the global economy: it is monomaniacally obsessed with *growth* as being the only possible solution to every problem, and given this mindset, the government is incapable of pricing in all the external costs because this would eliminate the profits that the government taxes for its own revenues.

The idea that what we really need is not *growth*, but *Degrowth*, is incomprehensible to government regardless of its ideology or form. Governments depend on *endless growth at any cost* to fund their revenues as much as monopolist corporations.

We might also ask: doesn't government have enough to do just trying to manage everything that's already on its plate, from national security to filling potholes? Why not acknowledge that government is the wrong system and wrong structure to operate a self-organizing, anti-fragile system that is designed to do what government isn't designed to do?

So no, the government can't do what CLIME can do, for all these systemic reasons. I explain all this in greater detail in my books *Resistance, Revolution, Liberation: A Model for Positive Change* and *Pathfinding Our Destiny*.

My hope is that enlightened government leadership will recognize the benefits of CLIME. A self-organizing system that pays its members with its own currency to do work neither the public nor for-profit sectors can perform would be doing the government and the nation a great service. The government could collect taxes on the CLIME wages and transactions, so why wouldn't it welcome this expansion of value, employment, and tax revenues? Does it really make more sense to borrow trillions of dollars, burdening future generations, to pay individuals to *shoot baskets alone* rather than give them an opportunity to belong to a productive, community-enriching system that pays its own way?

An unenlightened (i.e. self-serving) government leadership would naturally fear CLIME for two reasons: (1) since it couldn't control the CLIME currency, it couldn't impoverish CLIME members with inflation the way it impoverishes the rest of the populace; and (2) the CLIME groups, though local, might band together into larger political groups that could advocate for all CLIME members, most of whom had no previous means to advance their interests. This advocacy on behalf of people who were previously powerless might threaten the dominance of the ruling elites.

But governments may have little choice in the matter if their national currencies lose all value and the populace demands the political right to establish CLIME groups and be paid with the CLIME currency.

Won't Robots and AI Do All the Work?

One heavily promoted forecast has robots and AI performing all the work humans once did, ushering in a golden age of leisure and freedom for humanity. If this is the future, then what's the point of even discussing community work or labor-backed currencies?

I dismantle this fantasy in my books *Money and Work Unchained* and *Will You Be Richer or Poorer? Profit, Power and A.I. in a Traumatized World*. As a quick summary of why this techno-fantasy in disconnected from reality:

- Most work is not profitable and will never be profitable. This is why the vast majority of human work is unpaid. Profitable work is only a thin slice of all human labor, and it only exists in wealthy nations with a class of high earners who have the money to pay for profitable services. People who walk a mile to collect water do not have the money to pay for a costly drone to do the work, and they will never have enough money to buy costly robots because they have little access to the global marketplace or value to offer that marketplace.

- Robots and AI are not free, so they can only perform profitable work, i.e. work that generates enough revenue to pay for all the costs of buying, operating and maintaining the robots. Robots will never be free, regardless of the technology employed to construct them. All the parts and components must be fabricated using energy and materials which will never be free. Energy will never be free (see below), the replacement and maintenance of energy systems will never be free, transport will never be free, maintenance and repair will never be free, and so on.

- As noted previously, alternative energy such as wind and solar is not *renewable*, it is *replaceable*, meaning the entire installed base has to be replaced every 20-25 years, at enormous expense. Batteries do not last very long, either, and recycling them is extremely costly. Disposing of unrecyclable worn-out 30-foot long fiberglass windmill blades is already a costly problem.

- Despite hundreds of billions of dollars invested, alternative "replaceable" energy provides about 3% of all the energy humanity consumes—basically *background noise*. The idea that energy will soon be abundant and free is pure fantasy.

- Global manufacturers cannot even make clothes washers and dryers that function for more than a few years before they require expensive repairs; why will robots be any more durable than other manufactured goods, all of which end up in the landfill within a few years? If it costs $300 for a cheap circuit board and another $200 in labor to repair a failed clothes dryer that cost $700 new, what will it cost to repair a failed $10,000 robot?

- Robots are not universal machines that function equally well anywhere on the planet. The vast majority of robots need flat surfaces and ideal weather conditions. In the real world, robots are either toys for the wealthy, government weapons systems, or tools for corporations to eliminate the costs of human labor as a means of increasing their profits.

- Robots must be recharged and maintained, expensive processes outside the developed, wealthy economies. Imagine a fleet of costly drones programmed to collect all the thousands of pieces of trash on remote tropic islands. Who will pay people to collect the drones that fail? Who will transport the energy sources to recharge all the drones? Who will pay to transport the drones to the remote islands? What will be done with the trash collected?

- Where will the trillions of dollars needed to fund this *replaceable* energy system that must be rebuilt every generation come from? As explained previously, the current money system is unsustainable. Once asset bubbles pop and central bank currencies lose value, there will be less money to spend, not more.

In other words, robots and AI are the icing on the cake of fossil fuels and an unsustainable financial system that creates money out of thin air but cannot create energy, metals, circuit boards, food, potable water, fertile soil, etc. out of thin air.

The Real World of Corporate AI: Exploitive, Parasitic, Socially Destructive

In the techno-fantasy, robots and AI magically arise to serve humanity based on the belief that the global spread of incredibly positive technology is inevitable. All obstacles will be effortlessly overcome by technology.

In the real world, technologies spread because governments and corporations invest in the research and development and companies commercialize products to make a profit.

The factories and labs to manufacture robots and program AI are owned by profit-maximizing corporations, and this is why the vision of everyone paying for robots and AI is so heavily promoted: the owners of the companies are hoping to become immensely wealthy by selling robots and AI to the world.

In the real world, AI technology has generated the dominance of social media, digital entertainment and Internet search by a handful of corporations, collectively known as *Big Tech*. As Marx observed, the most profitable arrangement is a monopoly or cartel, where customers have few other options and so the monopolies can control price to their advantage.

Big Tech has harnessed AI (machine learning algorithms, etc.) to dominate markets and increase profits. These algorithms are known as *black box* technologies because no one outside the corporation can look inside to see what they're actually doing. Since the corporations are privately owned, all the AI is secret.

The biggest source of Big Tech's profits is the data it collects from its users. This immense flow of data is their most valuable asset, since advertisers will pay a lot of money to learn about individual customers and then target them based on their search and shopping habits. These technologies enable the owners of the data to influence customers' behavior based on their profile: the owners of all the data don't just influence your purchases by targeting marketing, they influence your political and social opinions by manipulating what you see on news feeds and what's being withheld so you won't see it.

In effect, the Big Tech companies have become de facto *quasi-sovereign states*, i.e. the digital-empire equivalent of governments, because they have global networks of surveillance, censorship, data collection and behavioral influence that are larger than any government. Since the corporate leadership is like a private monarchy, there is no democratic control at all by users or citizens. These companies are literally powers unto themselves.

As Susan Benesch, a faculty associate at Harvard University's Berkman Klein Center for Internet & Society observed in a July 2020 *Guardian.com* (UK) article, "They have taken on the task of defining unacceptable speech, which is a quasi-sovereign power... and we the public have no opportunity to contribute to the decision-making, as would be the case if the decisions were being made by a government."

In the same article, University of Virginia media studies professor Siva Vaidhyanathan said, "The root of Facebook is the fact that it is a global intrusive surveillance system that leverages all that behavioral data to target both ads and non-ad content at us."

These companies' AI-automated algorithms decide what you're allowed to see on news feeds, what you're not allowed to see, and also what's being promoted at the top of the search results. How the algorithms decide what to promote and what to hide is a closely held secret, yet what we see and read has an enormous effect on our opinions and beliefs, which ultimately influence our votes in elections. All this is done with the explicit goal of *maximizing profits by any means available*. The social harm done isn't measured and therefore it doesn't matter.

As a result, these privately owned AI-based companies are not just immensely profitable; they wield more political influence than traditional political advocacy groups because (1) they control search results and news feeds, and (2) their cash hoards are so stupendous that they can effectively lobby to restrict government oversight of their monopolies. The feedback loop is ominous: since government regulators are stymied by Big Tech lobbying, the platforms are in effect protected from any democratic control exerted by the citizenry of their nominal "home nation," not to mention the citizenry they influence in other nations.

Unlike the old monopolies like Standard Oil, the Big Tech platforms *are the media*, so there's little left in the system to balance their skyrocketing power. They influence the opinions and beliefs of their billions of users, the government's regulatory agencies, and the electoral results.

Rather than enhance human leisure and freedom, the Big Tech platforms are exploiting human psychology: social media addicts its users to anger and polarization, which increase "engagement" (the time users spend online) and thus profits. As for freedom, Big Tech's control of search and news feeds corrupts democracy to enrich the owners of Big Tech corporations.

Rather than usher in some idealized golden age, AI in the hands of profit-maximizing monopolies is a *socially destructive, parasitic activity.* It exploits human weaknesses, encourages destructive addictions, profits from data collected on every aspect of individuals' lives and fatally weakens democracy and the citizens' right to place limits on corporate power.

The sole purpose of their activity is to maximize their own profits, and the sole purpose of those paying billions of dollars for Big Tech's user data is to promote *over-consumption of the planet's scarce resources*—once again, *socially destructive, parasitic activity* that lays waste to the planet to profit corporate owners.

This is the reality, not some techno-fantasy based on magical thinking.

CLIME's AI: Level the Playing Field, Empower Every CLIME Group

As I explained before, the larger purpose of CLIME's use of AI isn't to make trillion-dollar corporations even more powerful; instead its purpose is to level the playing field by eliminating privilege, treating every individual equally and providing equal access to technological tools for all CLIME members.

This is of course anathema to corporations seeking monopolies in robotics and AI. Socially useful activity has no value whatsoever in their mad rush to maximize profits by any means available.

We must also ask: when was it ordained that humans must bow down to profit-maximizing corporations' view of how technology should be used? When did we forget that humans don't have to obey the supposed dictates of technology? If technology lessens the risks of dangerous work and improves productivity, then there's certainly room for humans to work with technology. But the techno-fantasy of a workless world of leisure is one of implicit servitude to technology and those who own it, as if we have no choice in the matter.

For any number of reasons, we might choose to limit the uses of robotics and AI. Adopting robotics and AI is a matter of choice, with a great many factors to consider. Yet to the techno-fantasy true believers, humans are nothing more than consumers of technologies owned by Big Tech monopolies, consumers who will gladly trade positive social roles for the meaningless, purposeless wasteland of over-consumption.

The AI in CLIME will create income, power and equality for the many rather than profits and privileges for the few. Rather than being owned by secretive monopolies, the AI tools of CLIME will be open source and owned by the membership, for the benefit of the membership and the greater world beyond. How each CLIME group makes use of technology is up to the members; the priority isn't maximizing profits and consumption but *doing more with less* (Degrowth) in pursuit of socially useful activity, i.e. *sharing the wealth of a shrinking planet.*

Why Not Let Corporations Make a Profit Doing All These Things?

There's one more standard objection to cover: since markets solve all problems, why not let corporations make a profit doing whatever needs to be done?

The basic thought is: if something is worth doing, it will generate a profit for some smart individual or company, so if we free the marketplace so people can make a profit, all valuable work will get done because the profit motive will inspire solutions. Therefore we don't need your CLIME system; we just need to remove everything that constrains markets. The unspoken assumption here is that if there's no profit to be reaped, it isn't worth doing.

However, the mother walking a mile to fetch water for her family would beg to differ: there is no way carrying the water for her will ever be profitable because she has no money to spend on services like carrying water. Yet the water she carries is essential to the survival of her family, so it's extremely valuable to her.

I've already pointed out other problems with the simplistic "the profit motive will fix everything" ideology—the external costs (pollution, etc.) dumped into humanity's shared biosphere isn't calculated in the price, and neither are future costs (cancer from smoking tobacco, recycling all the dead lithium-ion batteries, etc.).

The other problem is that what sounds good on a small scale—improving everyone's living standards by giving them access to the global economy—becomes exploitive when global capital—corporations, private equity, hedge funds, financiers, etc.—can corrupt or exploit local markets and economies.

For example, global companies can dump used clothing from the wealthy countries that have too much clothing into local economies. This may lower the cost of clothing a bit, but it also destroys the local businesses that sew clothing: they can't compete with used clothing from the West.

Global corporations are experts at *arbitrage*, the ability to skim a profit by exploiting differences in the value of currencies, labor, capital, etc. For example, a global corporation will promise to build a factory in return for low taxes and lax environmental standards. Once the tax benefits have been exploited, the company leaves just as quickly as it arrived.

The belief that markets are the solution to all problems is called *neoliberalism. Liberalizing economies* to free up labor, capital and innovation is an old idea, and so the new shiny version is called *neo* (a new form) liberalism.

The idea that removing barriers to markets and maintaining a stable currency are the best way to stimulate economic prosperity is an ancient one, going back to the Tang Dynasty in China (if not earlier) and Medieval Europe. Opening markets and lifting excessive tariffs on trade increases prosperity because small farmers and tradespeople can move their goods to markets where they fetch a higher price than the local markets near their homes. With these extra earnings in hand, they can buy tools to increase their productivity, increase the size of their animal herd, etc. As their earnings grow, they can afford luxuries made elsewhere, providing new sales and profits for other traders. A stable currency is essential because traders need to know that the money they're trading goods and services for will still be worth the same amount next month and next year.

But as I've explained throughout the book, markets can't solve everything, especially if they can't accurately price all the costs. There are social values that cannot be reduced to profits, for example, the value of maintaining local food production (i.e. *food security*). Markets also create false equivalents; for example, "farmed fish are equivalent to wild-caught fish" (false), "tree farms are the equivalent of old-growth forests" (false), etc.

In global markets, scarcity creates value, and over-supply pushes prices down. People who must walk to fetch water have no skills or products that are scarce in global markets, and there are few ways to get their products to distant markets. The ideological belief that markets will magically give everyone some scarce skill or product to sell is just another form of *magical thinking*. The reality is that global corporations pay very little for labor or resources and then reap all the profits.

The CLIME system will avoid these traps by creating its own stable currency and paying its members to perform useful work, whether it is profitable or not. These wages then enable each member to fulfill their own interests and ambitions. Since the CLIME system isn't dependent on global markets or corporations, no one in a CLIME group has to sell their labor or products for next to nothing: other CLIME groups are the market for goods and services created within CLIME.

(If those outside CLIME are willing to pay a fair price for goods produced within CLIME, then that's encouraged. The point here is no one within in CLIME is forced to sell their labor or products for next to nothing.)

Since everyone will earn a wage within CLIME, everyone will have the opportunity to save up some capital which they can invest in their own household or loan to others willing to pay interest.

The key point here is that CLIME's self-supporting markets for goods, services, labor and capital offer members all the benefits of free markets while protecting them from the exploitation that comes with dependence on global markets dominated by global corporations.

The conventional solutions boil down to three types of magical thinking: (1) governments can solve everything; (2) robots and AI will solve everything, and (3) markets will solve everything. While each of these solutions has a potentially positive role in the future, singly or together they don't solve the core problem, which is that each is incapable of leveling the playing field, providing equal opportunity and equitably sharing the diminishing resources of our planet. Only CLIME can accomplish these essential tasks, for only CLIME connects the dots between *values, processes and systems*.

To get a better sense of how CLIME would work in the real world, let's imagine that CLIME is up and running, and I'm joining the system for the first time. I don't mean an imaginary individual, I mean me, the author of this book that you've come to know through my personal history.

The idea here is to give you a taste of the day-to-day experience of working in the CLIME system. There is no way I can provide a detailed account in this snapshot; it required almost 50 pages in my book *A Radically Beneficial World* just to outline the system.

The first thing you'll notice is that even though I'm the creator of the system, I don't get any special privileges. I don't control the wealth of the system or its governance. I'm just like everyone else joining the system, because CLIME has no space for privilege—even for its founder.

An Imaginary Journey into CLIME

Here's my imagined first day in CLIME:

I find I have so many impressions in this busy first day that I don't know where to start. What struck me right away in visiting various CLIME groups was the *camaraderie*, the atmosphere of shared purpose, and for lack of a better word, *fun*. Not that the work was always fun—it was often hard and tedious—but it still felt as if the freedom and sharing were enjoyable, even if the work wasn't.

Whenever I've listened to those employed in the government/corporate world, all I've ever heard is complaints; everyone seems to dislike their job, their supervisor, and the entire set-up. They're only there because of their need for the paycheck. They control virtually nothing about their work or the organization, and their powerlessness drains them of life and joy.

In CLIME groups, everyone seems happier because everyone knows they can leave whatever they're doing now and join another group at any time—and if they can't find a group they like, they can start their own. Wherever they go in CLIME, they're guaranteed a wage, choices and voice in the running of the group they belong to.

Even though one of the group meetings I witnessed struck me as barely controlled chaos, everyone had a say. A vote was held and despite the grumbling by the losing side, everybody understood that if the losers felt strongly enough, they could quit and find another group more to their liking.

What I saw was people coming to terms with tradeoffs: were there enough good things about the project to outweigh the inevitable frictions? If not, your freedom to move was unlimited: your income and security were independent of any group or project.

It's clear that some people never stay in any group for long, as their expectations are never quite met. These vagabonds are on an endless voyage in search of the "perfect group" and "perfect project" and perhaps "perfect humans" in that perfect group. Maybe they'll find it, maybe they won't.

Then there's others who seem to be perfectly happy doing the same work they started when they first joined CLIME. Maybe they found the right fit the first time out. I'm guessing most members are somewhere in between these extremes, but there's room for everyone along the spectrum.

That's actually my lasting impression: there's room for everyone in CLIME, from those who find satisfaction in performing the same simple tasks day after day to those who are fired with ambition to change the world for the better. There's room for those who like stability and those who crave variety, for those happy with a steady paycheck and those who want to make more income—maybe a lot more income, because CLIME encourages members to have their own private enterprises that offer goods and services to CLIME groups and members.

There's even room for misfits like me who swing between wanting to change the world for the better and just wanting to do simple work like pulling weeds.

One other overwhelming impression is the sheer variety of groups and projects: there are so many to choose from, though fewer in sparsely populated areas, of course. I was surprised not just by the range of activities but by the diversity of the fields of endeavor, from traditional (teaching kids to ride ponies where equestrian skills are practical) to higher-tech (designing/building drone-mounted sensors to measure moisture content on biomass plots) to individual care (children and the elderly) to systemic advances (software modules to add basic pension plans to CLIME).

And the diversity didn't stop at the paid-labor projects; some groups sponsored unpaid/volunteer efforts that didn't meet CLIME standards for paid work such as street theatre and neighborhood rodeo events.

There was also a variety of sizes and styles of groups. I saw one that chose to stay small—a dozen members--and have only one project: teaching children art skills in an after-school program. Other groups had hundreds of members and coordinated with other large groups to tackle major projects—repurposing abandoned retail spaces, constructing dedicated bikeways, etc.

I was also struck by the attention paid to meeting the automated requirements for verification. People had caught on that if the rules were ignored or given short shrift, the money immediately stopped flowing to individuals and groups. I witnessed more than one conflict resolved (not always good-naturedly) by someone declaring, "These are the rules that we all have to follow. If you don't like them, leave." The human desire for privilege and exemptions is eternal, but "the rules are the rules" seemed to be accepted as necessary.

Another surprise was the "that's the way it goes sometimes" acceptance of groups failing or being dissolved for non-compliance. The only way to truly be anti-fragile is to accept failures as a necessary part of the process, and it was interesting to see how failure was handled.

My guide for the day was Rose, one of the CLIME members who volunteers to show newcomers how CLIME works by taking them through a typical day of CLIME activities. Rose was in her 30s with two children; she'd first become interested in CLIME because she was seeking better childcare and education options for her kids. She'd started in a childcare project but found she had a knack for management and accounting, so she'd eventually joined a group that helped new groups learn the reporting requirements and understand the balance sheets the CLIME system automatically produced for each group. Her husband worked in a large group renovating an abandoned multi-story commercial building into housing units for CLIME members.

I found it interesting that Rose also had her own home-based business helping other CLIME members with home-based businesses set up basic accounting systems. She reported that her venture was a natural outcome of meeting so many people in CLIME who had a side business as a means of earning more money. While CLIME members only get paid for work performed in approved projects/groups, the CLIME marketplace encouraged buying and selling of goods and services created by CLIME members in their own private enterprises. The basic idea is to increase the range of goods and services available to members and to increase the productivity of the entire CLIME system.

Our first stop of the day was to an old industrial site *brown-field* project that the CLIME software had flagged as abandoned. The group that proposed the project had intended to clean up debris left by the demolition of the old warehouse, test the soil for contaminants and then proceed with planting whatever was needed—either cover crops to absorb the contaminants, or if the soil was clean, vegetables and food-forest trees.

When the automated software flagged any project, it randomly chose an auditing team from people in nearby groups to anonymously investigate conditions on the ground. Was the group performing the work it claimed to be doing? Was there evidence of progress being made?

Rose and I rode our bicycles to the site and noted some evidence of work having been done in the past—debris had been collected into piles—but there was no one on site and no signs of any recent work. Rose snapped a few photos with her phone and filed a brief report.

"Looks like the project ran out of steam," she commented. "It happens a lot. People drop out, the group took on more than they could handle--those are common reasons. But everyone learned something and hopefully they moved on to another group. And maybe a more established group will pick up where they left off. It still looks like a good project."

Our next stop happened to be the first group that Rose joined as a new member of CLIME. This group focused solely on childcare, and had a handful of projects serving this purpose. I was drawn to the outdoor area used to introduce young children to gardening and raising chickens by engaging them in simple tasks. I saw one young boy excitedly shout "I found one!" as he picked a green bean from a tangle of climbing vines, and within the controlled chaos of the garden area it was clear that work and play were being combined to connect what the kids ate for lunch with the earth and animals that produced the food.

This group's leadership was meeting for a specific purpose: to hear the appeal of a member who'd been caught exaggerating his work hours to boost his pay. The slogan posted on walls is "Anyone who steals from CLIME steals from every one of us." The applicant was waiting nervously outside the converted warehouse space that served as the group's headquarters, and Rose motioned me to follow her. She sat down beside the member and asked him what was going on. "I messed up," he confessed. "I padded my hours."

Rose was mildly sympathetic. "Lots of people are tempted to try, but they always get caught. Then they learn it's not worth it."

The applicant nodded and asked, "Think I'll get a second chance?"

"Unless you messed up by not doing the work, I'd say yes."

"No, I did the work," he assured us. "I always got good ratings."

"Then you'll probably just get a warning, and of course the automatic reduction in your reputation ranking. Nobody can dodge that."

"Yeah," he said, and then shrugged. "But I can earn back my old ranking, right?"

"Of course," Rose replied. "Everybody here wants you to earn it back."

After we left, Rose explained, "It's really common for newbies to test the system by fudging this or padding that. Since everything has to be verified, it's pretty hard to get away with any cheating. Everyone is trained to have zero tolerance, because once cheating becomes the norm, the group will be defunded and we all lose our reputation rankings."

After greeting some friends in the garden project, Rose turned to me and said, "There are lots of childcare groups of course, but this is one of the best. Parents choose this group as one of the top picks." The flash of friendly competition was inspirational because it showed that competition pressured weaker groups to improve their performance and kept top groups on their toes.

I also learned that the peer-to-peer reputation ranking system was self-policing, because anyone found exaggerating a rating or verification as a favor to a friend, etc., would lose their own ranking, so the incentives were to be honest with every verification entered into the system. Members verified other members in their group, interactions with other groups, and customers rated every group that they bought goods and services from.

Our next stop was the big construction project Rose's husband worked on, a multi-story commercial building that had long been abandoned and was being renovated into living spaces for CLIME members.

As Rose explained, the project financing was complicated, as it required the cooperation of local government, CLIME-peer-to-peer financing and some non-CLIME conventional-economy investment. The local government was willing to deed the property to a consortium of CLIME groups because it had been empty and hadn't paid any property taxes for years. There were no prospects for renting it for its former use—office space—and so the local government accepted the unconventional deal offered by the CLIME group consortium: the city would accept all tax payments in the CLIME cryptocurrency, relax certain requirements for parking, approve use of recycled materials, and deed ownership to the CLIME consortium for a nominal fee. For the city, the deal was a no-brainer: either let the property decay and be responsible for the eyesore, or deed it to the largely self-funding CLIME consortium.

Conventional capital wanted to invest because CLIME housing projects had a history of stability: since CLIME members had guaranteed incomes, they could afford the modest rent charged by the CLIME consortium. Since CLIME enables peer-to-peer lending, the consortium was able to borrow a substantial amount from individual members who wanted to invest in a CLIME project.

Given the extent of the CLIME economy and its systemic goal of reducing consumption and conserving resources, the consortium was able to source a great deal of perfectly usable recycled and refurbished materials for the construction project.

Donning battered red hardhats, Rose and I entered the jobsite and found her husband TJ, a lithe carpenter wearing a heavily decaled hardhat and a well-worn tool belt. Given my own decades of construction experience, the main challenge was readily visible: where each floor of the old office building had a single central block of restrooms and a bar sink in the office kitchenette, converting the floor to residential units required a massive expansion of plumbing and electrical systems to add bathrooms and kitchens to every unit. This required chipping out parts of concrete floors and adding spaces for new plumbing pipes and electrical conduits. The heating and cooling systems needed work to improve their efficiency, and the roof had to be converted to a rooftop garden and recreational space.

After returning to her group's office at the end of a busy day, Rose asked which groups I was thinking of joining. Glancing at my work experience (minus my role in creating CLIME, of course), she commented, "They could use you on TJ's project."

I said that while that project was appealing in its scale and use of recycled materials, I was also drawn to a group planting food forests, the project assembling off-grid direct-current solar powered systems from CLIME-sourced parts, and also to another project that was designing and coding a CLIME pension module that every group could add.

Though I didn't explain this to Rose, I'd long seen the lack of a pension plan as a weakness in CLIME, but had set it aside as a complex topic that needed more attention than would be possible in my outline of CLIME. So I was excited that a group was developing the necessary software to address that need.

After listing my interests, I smiled wryly and confessed, "But to tell the truth, sometimes I just want to pull weeds and spread compost," and Rose laughed. "Me, too. When I have a break, I still love getting out there with the kids in the garden."

     *   *   *

I hope this brief sketch offers a glimpse of the more sustainable, fulfilling, creative, adaptable and happier world that CLIME would enable. There's nothing holding us back from making it a reality.

Charles Hugh Smith

September 2020